MAGIC, WITCHCRAFT, AND RELI

California State University Sacramento **Revised 2nd Edition** Edited by Liam D. Murphy California Sta

Edited by Liam D. Murphy **California State University Sacramento** Edited by Liar

Bassim Hamadeh, CEO and Publisher

Kassie Graves, Director of Acquisitions and Sales

Jamie Giganti, Senior Managing Editor

Miguel Macias, Senior Graphic Designer

David Miano, Senior Specialist Acquisitions Editor

Natalie Lakosil, Senior Licensing Manager

Kaela Martin and Chelsey Schmid, Associate Editors

Kat Ragudos, Interior Designer

Cover image copyright © by Depositphotos / jlcst.

Printed in the United States of America

ISBN: 978-1-5165-1095-5 (pbk) / 978-1-5165-1096-2 (br)

 cognella® | ACADEMIC PUBLISHING

CONTENTS

Preface to the Revised Second Edition   ix

A Note to Instructors   xv

Introduction to the Revised Second Edition   1

Section One: Religion, Controversy, and Tradition Under Fire

Introduction   8

Article 1: Americans Switch Faiths Often   13
David Duprey

Article 2: Teens Serious About Religion   17
MSNBC.COM

Article 3: European Unity Tested Over Crucifixes in Classroom   21
Victor L. Simpson

Article 4: In Final Interview, Cardinal Says Church 200 Years Out of Date   25
Naomi O'Leary

Article 5: Vatican Official Calls Atheist Theories "Absurd"   27
MSNBC.COM

Article 6: Atheist Church Split: Sunday Assembly and Godless Revial's "Demoninational Chasm"   29
HUFFINGTONPOST.COM

Article 7: Christians Counter Atheists—On London Buses   31
Akira Suemori

Article 8: Transgender Mormons Struggle to Feel at Home, in Religion 33
Peggy Fletcher Stack

Discussion Questions 36

Further Readings 36

Section Two: Transcending Science

||||||||||||||||||||||||||||||||||||||||||||||||||||||||||||||||||||||||||||||||||||||||||||||||||||||||||||||

Introduction 40

Article 9: God and Science: An Inner Conflict 43
Robin Lloyd

Article 10: Televangelist Warns of Evolution Doomsday 47
Information Liberation

Article 11: Ghost Sightings Could Just Be Hallucinations Caused By Mold, Say Researchers 49
Robyn Pennacchia

Article 12: Inside Zombie Brains: Sci-Fi Teaches Science 51
Elizabeth Landau

Discussion Questions 56

Further Readings 56

Section Three: Magical Culture

||||||||||||||||||||||||||||||||||||||||||||||||||||||||||||||||||||||||||||||||||||||||||||||||||||||||||||||

Introduction 60

Article 13: Believers Flock to Virgin Mary Statue "Crying" Red Tears 67
Rich Pedroncelli

Article 14: How Walt Disney Made America into a Magic Kingdom 69
Gil Troy

Article 15: Why Babies (and Perhaps All of Us) Care About Magic   73
Susana Martinez-Conde

Article 16: Is Religion Good for Children?   77
Mark Joseph Stern

Discussion Questions   82

Further Readings   82

Section Four: Living with the Evil Dead

Introduction   86

Article 17: CNN Reporters Attacked by Ghosts Live on Air!   91
Moviepilot

Article 18: There are Tribes of "Vampire" People in New Orleans   93
John Edgar Browning

Article 19: Suck Fest   97
Jonah Spangenthal-Lee

Article 20: Why are Zombies the New Black?   99
Cole Eckhardt

Discussion Questions   102

Further Readings   102

Section Five: Fear in the Witching Hour

Introduction   106

Article 21: Mob Kills Witchcraft Couple   113
Bongani Hans

Article 22: African Children Denounced as Witches by Christian Pastors   115
Katharine Houreld

Article 23: Mobs Lynch Witches in Haiti for Spreading Cholera Epidemic   119
The Sydney Morning Herald

Article 24: Catholic Bishops: More Exorcists Needed   121
Rachel Zoll

Article 25: Vatican Denounces Group's Claim of Seeing the Virgin Mary
More Than 40,000 Times as "Work of the Devil"   125
Daily Mail Online

Article 26: Blood of Pope John Paul II Stolen in Possible "Satanic" Theft   127
Nick Squires

Article 27: Is Harry Potter in Cahoots with Hell?   129
Drew Zahn

Article 28: Woman Beaten to Death After Being Accused of   133
of Witchcraft on Facebook
Annalee Newitz

Discussion Questions   134

Further Readings   134

Section Six: The Real Witches of Today

Introduction   138

Article 29: Pagans Are on the March   145
Zoe Brennan

Article 30: Salem Warlock Blends Business with Sorcery   151
Billy Baker

Article 31: Police Say They Plan to Arrest Satanic Temple Members   155
Who Protested Westboro Baptist Church
Hunter Stuart

Article 32: Satanic Temple Leader "Very Happily Surprised" By Support   157
for Oklahoma Monument
Carla Hinton

Discussion Questions   160

Further Readings   160

Index   163

PREFACE

To the Revised Second Edition

In 2008, I was approached by Cognella Academic Publishing about developing a new text for courses on the anthropology of religion, magic, and witchcraft. At that time, my first thought was that the last thing a saturated textbook market needed was yet another volume for undergraduates to wade through. As I began to consider the matter more closely, however, it dawned on me that there were still many facets of religion, the supernatural, the occult, and the paranormal in the United States and elsewhere that had yet to be mined for publication.

In particular, I considered the filing cabinet drawer in my university office, stuffed to overflowing with photocopied articles and printed Internet news reports about religion and religious phenomena. For some years, I had been collecting these in order to (one day) rifle through them, on the hunt for new material and "real world" examples that might be insinuated into my courses. Even when I found no way to incorporate them into my lecture notes, for some period of time these articles—with such sensationalist titles as "Catholic Bishops: More Exorcists Needed," and "Mob Kills Witchcraft Couple"—would be tacked to a small notice board on the wall outside my office door. For my efforts, I have occasionally been rewarded with a student comment or e-mail about these articles, and I have often been surprised by the ways in which various newsworthy events have tapped into the imaginations of students with little prior exposure.

Philosopher Marshall McLuhan famously quipped that "the medium is the message." It may be true that some parts of the world (or, more likely, some segments of U.S. society) are entering a post-religious age of sorts, but you would never know it from the copious body of popular writing about the mysterious domain of supernatural beliefs and practices disseminated in print and online. If there is anything to notions of supply and demand, then surely there must be an ongoing interest among the non-specialist and even non-church-going public in those anecdotal traces of religiosity that suffuse today's media. The perennial popularity of mainstream films and television shows that exploit these in the interests of popular entertainment and advertising revenue lends still more support to the idea that many Americans (and almost certainly others) are shifting away from an attitude of fidelity and respect for religion and toward one of persistent curiosity about the paranormal. While it is clear that many millions of Americans continue to anchor their sense of self and cultural identity in religion, this level of commitment can no longer be taken for granted. Even when the millennial generation seeks out religious experience in earnest, it is seldom with the sectarian or doctrinal leanings of their grandparents. Like it or not, the attitude toward religion is changing in this country, and only time will tell whether the many institutions of our religious culture will be reinvigorated in the new millennium.

However, I do not wish to be misunderstood. To say that religion is changing is a long way from saying that it is disappearing. Despite the many claims of social scientists and (occasionally) anti-religion militants, "secularization"—the purging of religion from civil society—is hardly taking place. Rather, we seem to have entered an era that is increasingly "de-churched"; a time in which fragments of belief, tradition, and practice are variously embraced, discarded, or swapped out for one another in a free marketplace of religious ideas and possibilities. The prospects for innovation spawned by the new, media-driven culture around us seem to drive, rather than destroy, ongoing interest in religion in the modern United States.

Moreover, there is another sense in which religion cannot be said to be disappearing from public life. Decades ago, sociologist Robert Bellah wrote of the emergence of a late-modern world in which a large variety of civic and cultural institutions were effectively meeting the social and psychological needs and purposes of religion without actually being religious, as the word is normally construed. Thus, nation states, professional sports, and a host of cultural associations of one kind or another all embrace and embody rituals, values, and institutions that in a very real sense "are" religion. Perhaps better than any other example, the nation as an "imagined community" (to use anthropologist Benedict Anderson's phrase) incorporates a wider variety of values, creeds, meanings, rituals, commitments, symbols, heroes, organizations, and roles that resemble religion—all without the apparent centrality of a creator God (although this has always been the subject of much dispute and controversy). What is the general presidential election if not the central collective ritual of the nation, observed at prescribed intervals and laden with pomp and ceremony? What are congressmen and senators if not the chief priests of the state? What are the Declaration of Independence and U.S.

Constitution if not the scriptures of the nation? And who are George Washington, Abraham Lincoln, and Martin Luther King, Jr. if not the eternal heroes of the nation (much like saints in Christianity)? More prosaically, consider the vast armies of *Star Trek* and anime fans that routinely dress in costume; gather at national and international conferences; devour publications, films, and television series; and generally inhabit a world of signification that overlaps but is not isomorphic with broader U.S. and global societies. For any probing analysis of U.S. society, these examples are important—they point to the way in which religion must be thought of as a set of social processes and activities that are collectively much greater than the narrow definition we usually give it. Whether or not their authors have thought through these issues is, in a sense, beside the point. The many articles published on the topics of religion, the occult (a term widely used to describe secretive supernatural events, actions, and institutions), and the paranormal (another popular umbrella term generally used to describe transcendent phenomena without reference to religion) are responding to a public hunger that seems never quite satiated. It is in exploration of this craving through an anthropological lens that I devote the revised second edition of *Magic, Witchcraft, and Religion in the Media.*

My goals in this edition are straightforward. First, to update the collection of readings to reflect new developments and interest in the mass print media concerning religion, spirituality, and the paranormal (these terms themselves deserve some unpacking, which I will do in the introduction). This accumulation of news stories has, if anything, proliferated over the last few years. My largest problem in assembling a new collection has been to decide which articles deserved inclusion in a revised second edition. I finally settled on the thirty-two selections included in this volume. Some of these are retained from the previous editions. Others are new and represent developments I feel are worthy of discussion in this, the second decade of a new century. Some inclusions are relatively lengthy and thoughtful; others are relatively short and to the point. All should provoke reflection and—I hope—lively conversation.

As with the articles included in the first edition, I admit to having little method in deciding which to use in the revised second, other than a dogged determination to keep it interesting. I discovered most through many hours of online subject searches and perusal of various websites and have included only a fraction of those articles I came across. I make no secret of the fact that these articles were chosen in the first instance because they suited my personal and pedagogical interests, and not because I had in mind a well-rounded reader in which many religious traditions were represented. Of the thirty-six selections, for instance, science and the supernatural, Roman Catholicism, voodoo, African witchcraft, vampires, and Satanism receive their fair share of attention, while there is little or no mention of Islam, Hinduism, or Native American traditions, among others. Some might consider the absence of these traditions a large oversight, but I do not claim to be comprehensive in the general sense of that word. In theory, I could go on indefinitely—adding article upon article to subsequent editions. But to do so would be impractical, in terms both of volume, length, and cost.

Another goal of this revised second edition is to introduce students to important themes in the anthropology of religion by grouping these articles into six categories, each of which reflects a common theme. These sections have been revised since the first edition in order to make room for different articles, and each is prefaced by a discussion of the overall significance of the events, persons, and circumstances elaborated in the articles. It has been my intention to write each of these pieces in a conversational tone and without the many academic citations, independent clauses, caveats, footnotes, and other signs of academic enterprise. As with the first edition, my hope for the revised second is that the relative informality of my approach will prove appealing both to instructors and students, many of whom are accustomed to more ponderous, albeit more sophisticated, textbooks and readers.

Completion of this reader has not been a solitary undertaking, and I must thank Jamie Giganti, Dr. David Miano, Monika Dziamka, Miguel Macias, Jennifer Bowen Levine, Dani Skeen, Danielle Menard, Claire Yee, and the staff at Cognella Academic Publishing for all their hard work on this revised second edition. I am also very grateful to the many journalists, editorialists, and production staff of the various media outlets who have supplied the "grist" for my mill. This book is dedicated with fondness and gratitude to the many students, past and present, who have taken my course, Anthropology 13: Magic, Witchcraft, and Religion, which I have taught since 2002 at California State University, Sacramento. Over the years, they have given me the priceless opportunity to broaden my own horizons in the interests of teaching general education—for this I cannot thank them enough.

Liam D. Murphy
August 2015

Further Readings

1. Benedict Anderson. *Imagined Communities: Reflections on the Origins and Spread of Nationalism*, Revised Edition. London: Verso, 2006.
   A now-classic exposition of how the origins of national consciousness and community are rooted in literacy, changes to official religion, and the global spread of empires since the fifteenth century.
2. Robert N. Bellah. *The Broken Covenant: American Civil Religion in Time of Trial*, Second Edition. University of Chicago Press, 1992.

In this work, Bellah, a renowned sociologist of religion, discusses how the institutions, values, and perspectives embedded in U.S. civil society mirror many aspects of "traditional" US religion.

3. Steve Bruce. *God Is Dead: Secularization in the West.* Chichester, UK: Wiley-Blackwell Press, 2002.

This book outlines Bruce's perspective that various events and processes (especially the popularity of Eastern and "new" religions, political scandals, and the advances of science) are now undermining the traditional authority and status of Euro-American Christianity in the twenty-first century.

A NOTE TO INSTRUCTORS

T he editorial text and articles contained in *Magic, Witchcraft, and Religion in Media*, Revised Second Edition, are written in an accessible manner that should appeal to non-anthropology majors and an educated public. Still, the volume is intended to be used in conjunction with other course materials and texts in the context of classroom instruction. Along these lines, I believe that students taking introductory and general education courses in the anthropology of religion will benefit more from the volume if they are familiar with some of the key concepts of social and cultural anthropology (for instance, culture, ritual, relativism, and ethnocentrism, as these have been defined by anthropologists). In addition, it would be of some help (but not indispensable) for students enrolled in these courses to have some general knowledge of the colonial foundations of anthropology as a discipline, together with some vantage on how non-Western peoples have been viewed, historically, by Europeans and European diasporas. Instructors will also note that in my section introductions I have largely avoided lengthy digressions into anthropological theory and the pantheon of scholars generally discussed in anthropology of religion classes. *Mostly* absent is discussion of such luminaries as E.B. Tylor, James Frazer, Bronislaw Malinowski, E.E. Evans-Pritchard, Emile Durkheim, Max Weber, and Anthony Wallace. The work of these and many others is largely (though not completely) implicit in my brief discussions—each of which is intended to expose "classic" observations even while avoiding the perceived tedium of names, dates, and theories. Occasionally, names and works are cited in the Further Readings sections. To reiterate, ideally these introductions will supplement, rather than replace, a traditional textbook on the subject.

Finally, it is my hope and intention that the articles presented here provide a focus for vibrant classroom discussion. To this end, I have included a series of discussion questions and revised and annotated further readings at the conclusion of each section. Admittedly, there is little rigorous method to which works were selected for inclusion in the Further Readings sections, but I have both suggested supplementary texts by any researchers mentioned in the introductions and endeavored to present something of a mix of academic and popular material. In addition, the second edition contains an index, which I hope will assist readers in more effectively using the volume.

LDM

INTRODUCTION

To the Revised Second Edition

T he power and influence of religion in shaping U.S. history cannot be understated. From the earliest days of settlement by Puritans and other "non-conformists" to the deism and freemasonry of eighteenth-century elites (among them several "founding fathers"); to the powerful currents of African religion kept alive throughout long years of slavery; to the influx of Catholic and Jewish Europeans in the nineteenth century and from other parts of the world in the twentieth (all of whom brought their own distinctive ethnic and religious traditions with them); and to the efflorescence of "new religions" and fascination with the so-called paranormal that has emerged since the end of the Second World War, the United States has at once treasured and kept at arm's length its religious heritage. The First Amendment of the Constitution enshrines the idea that the government should not "establish" (that is, it should refrain from making "official") one form of religion to the subordination or exclusion of others, and this is commonly viewed as one of the corner-stones of American "freedom." Perhaps for this reason, there currently exists an extravagantly rich tapestry of faith worlds and practices considered by many to be a hallmark of American national culture. The articles throughout this volume illuminate some aspects of how religious diversity and change are treated in public discourse, as filtered by the print and electronic media.

Media coverage of events, personalities, and institutions often waits on dramatic developments or special moments, rather than on subtle changes or everyday activities, to tell the story of religion in America. For instance, the author has been called on at various points to shed light on such mysterious phenomena as "weeping statues" and ghost hunting, to forecast developments in the Catholic Church following the death of a

1

beloved Pope, to discuss the significance of Halloween ritual in modern society, and to identify the origin of Easter eggs.

This eclectic "laundry list" reflects a mercurial public interest in religion and **transcendent** phenomena—at least to the extent that these (the interests and the phenomena) evolve in new, thought-provoking, and apparently unpredictable ways.

How should we address this clear fascination that seems to defy traditional expectations of religious commitment by embracing a wide diversity of issues and interests, current and historical? The word transcendent is useful in this discussion because it points to a world of public interest that goes beyond well-circumscribed faith worlds per se; it indicates a widespread anticipation of, and intense curiosity about, the possibilities of existence outside the world of the everyday senses—a universe that literally merges with and transcends our own without being identical to it. Other terms might be used instead (among them, supernatural, spiritual, and paranormal), but most of these carry a certain amount of cultural baggage in already being connected to well-defined sets of belief. The term supernatural, for example, has been somewhat burdened by connotations of the primitive, superstitious, and illogical. The word transcendent is to this point not burdened by such expectations, and so is more useful for academic analysis. Many millions of Americans profess fascination with and a love of things transcendent (vampires, ghosts, and Halloween, for example) even when the thought of worshipping in a church makes them cringe. One need not be a professional student of the American landscape of region to notice that its diversity is not fixed, but is rather "on the move," with new ideas, rituals, and "traditions" coming into existence seemingly overnight and others disappearing just as quickly. There are potentially many patterns to be identified in this shifting vista of beliefs and institutions, but among the most significant are those that denote fundamental changes in how Americans perceive the role, status, and relevancy of a transcendent world in relation to human society.

This brings us to an important point. Useful as the term transcendent is, we cannot avoid the issue of what we mean by the term religion. How should we define the word in a way that is broad enough to encompass the many ideas we pack inside it? In teaching, I have often felt that I spend more time than necessary sifting through the various possible ways to untie the knot of religion, examining it from many angles: social, historical, cultural, political, psychological, and archaeological. The simple truth is that there is no universally accepted definition of religion, if for no other reason than because for many, many people, religion is synonymous with their most intimate assumptions about ultimate, universal reality. Put another way, for the faithful religion is not a belief system, historical epoch, or cultural construct—it is simply The Truth ... notwithstanding that there are many other people who have failed to embrace it.

For my purposes in this volume, however, and because I am a social scientist, I will treat religion as a social, cultural, and historical phenomenon. More specifically, we may define a religion (as opposed to the transcendent, which is a more inclusive term) as any social institution that possesses some or all of the following characteristics:

- recognizes and/or venerates transcendent beings, powers, and/or principles
- stipulates social and personal conventions, activities, and rituals that engage these transcendent beings, powers, and/or principles
- advances "sacred" narratives that describe the transcendent world and the place of humankind in relation to it
- upholds "sacred" values, dispositions, and subjective states that are appropriate and meaningful in the context of human relations with the transcendent world
- institutionalizes and regulates social relationships, hierarchies, and roles with the goal of sustaining and enhancing connections between humanity and the transcendent world

All the articles presented here address some aspect of the transcendent and most address some aspect of religion. This includes people, events, and concepts behind the terms magic and witchcraft—themselves the focus of much definitional wrangling (each of which will be defined in their section introductions). Again, remember that the word transcendent is intended to evoke the idea of a world that is conjoined with, but somehow different than, our own.

Bearing in mind these open-ended definitions, one might correctly infer that it is easy to talk at cross purposes when discussing transcendent and religious phenomena—easy to assume that we're speaking of the same thing, even when I have ritual practices in mind (that is, those shared, patterned activities involving extensive manipulation of symbols and performed at specific intervals) while the person I'm conversing with is thinking that religion is about belief in God or attendance at a church. Still, this complexity is perhaps inevitable given the plurality of our overall culture and conditions in the modern world more broadly. In the increasingly cosmopolitan society of early twenty-first-century America, religious and cultural pluralism are not only valued in and of themselves, but also function as a sort of ideological buffet. In ever-increasing numbers, Americans feel at liberty to explore different possibilities, indulge in new perspectives, and even cobble together their own visions of the universe based on an *à la carte* philosophy. In other words, what I mean by religion might well change over time based on my experience of the expanding social diversity all around us.

Often, this is a net positive. In teaching, I try across all my classes to strike a sanguine tone about how useful and enriching it is to be exposed to ways of knowing, thinking, and behaving that are unlike one's own. However, I would be less than candid if I didn't point out that this strength is also a liability. Among the most problematic aspects of religion is its tendency to serve as an important barometer of social difference. Too often the loftier, nobler goal of reuniting human beings with ultimate truth and purpose (the conceptual foundation of the word religion; Latin: *re-ligio*: to "re-connect") is supplanted with concerns of a more worldly nature and our baser drives: xenophobia, racism, sexism, ethnocentrism, and the intoxication of power. While denouncers of religious institutions may miss some of the more subtle beauties, ethics, joys, and profundities of commitment to a church or similar organization, they generally get it right when it comes to issues of corruption and moral hypocrisy: religion, just like all human institutions, beliefs, and practices, is prone to misuse. Moreover, because many religious worldviews distinguish the right from the wrong and the good from the evil, they very readily avail themselves of cultural processes of "othering." That is, religion is useful in the erection and support of "us versus them" forms of understanding around the world. This is especially the case when one's own cultural biases remain implicit when characterizing someone else's religion.

On this cautionary note, let us move now to the six sections in which slender slivers of media attention to these themes are explored. While many of the articles subsumed within these sections overlap, each reflects a particular perspective that is useful in thinking through an anthropological analysis of religion, the transcendent, magic, and witchcraft as viewed through the lens of U.S. (and occasionally international) media.

Further Readings

1. Talal Asad. *Genealogies of Religion: Discipline and Reasons of Power in Christianity and Islam*. Baltimore: John Hopkins University Press, 1993.
   A collection of well-known anthropologist Asad's essays on (primarily) Western religion and culture, including his famous response to Clifford Geertz's position on religion as a web of socially unifying symbols. Asad's general perspective is that the social, political, and economic conditions of the historical epoch "modernity" have ultimately defined what it means to have religion and be religious in Western societies.
2. Clifford Geertz. *Islam Observed: Religious Developments in Morocco and Indonesia*. University of Chicago Press, 1971.
   Though written nearly fifty years ago, **Islam Observed** remains among this prolific author's central contributions to understanding the cultural meaning of religion in two Muslim societies. In particular, the book showcases Geertz's famous interpretive method of ethnographic analysis.

3. George M. Marsden. *Fundamentalism and American Culture*. Oxford University Press, 2006.

   Marsden offers a rich exploration of the theology, history, and influence of the Christian fundamentalist movement in U.S. society. This work will be of special interest to students seeking to understand the role of conservative religious beliefs and institutions in twenty-first-century America.

RELIGION, CONTROVERSY, AND TRADITION UNDER FIRE

SECTION ONE
INTRODUCTION

As the world becomes ever more tightly knit by way of mass media and communications, digital technologies, rapid travel, and the innumerable intercultural encounters these bring, it has perhaps been inevitable that very different sets of cultural values and meanings have come into conflict with one another. With the possible exception of language, nowhere is this more apparent than in the domain of religion—which people tend to have very strong commitments to or opinions about. In the United States, we often assume that religious faith and acceptance of transcendent powers and beings are a matter of personal choice. Still early in the twenty-first century, Americans are, as we see in a pair of articles in this section, more willing to consider and reconsider their religious affiliations time and again, flitting among and flirting with options that seem more appealing at different stages of the life cycle.

Most of us would recognize that however laudable this ideal, it appears to be observed more in the breach than in the practice. In fact, social life in the United States and elsewhere is rife with disagreements that seem always poised to flare into controversies of national and international import. As the articles on classroom crucifixes and violence on buses attest, controversies have erupted in Europe over the status of explicitly religious symbols in the public sphere—particularly in classrooms and other state-run institutions. Perhaps the most acrimonious European debate in recent years has focused on the wearing of headscarves (*hijabs*) by Muslim women in France—a debate poised to become still more divisive after several 2015 terrorist attacks in Paris. In the United States, debate over the morality and legality of abortion is a perennial reminder of how deeply religion can penetrate national politics by way of the so-called "culture wars." Recent years have also witnessed sharp differences in religious conviction sparked by issues ranging from birth control to gay marriage to euthanasia to the content of middle and high school textbooks. From his deathbed, a Catholic cardinal prodded the Church to recommit itself to meeting these and other challenges posed by the contemporary world. "Why don't we rouse ourselves—are we afraid?" he warns. Still, more than traditional religion is at stake in the splintering of modern faith worlds. As another of the articles shows, even atheist churches have their own inner tensions and disagreements to resolve. The final article in section one focuses on a simmering controversy that has recently flared into media awareness within one of the best-known and most-powerful American "new religions": the Church of Jesus Christ, Latter-Day Saints (a.k.a. the Mormons).

Such disputes have been especially heated where matters of national security are perceived to be at stake. Acrimonious debate has also attended the erection of an Islamic center and mosque several city blocks away from ground zero in New York City—site of the September 11, 2001, attacks and considered by many New Yorkers and others to be sacred ground. This particular controversy took a still more bizarre turn when, in July 2010, a Floridian evangelical pastor, Terry Jones, made public his intentions to stage a Qur'an burning on the grounds of his small church in Gainesville—an event Jones asserted could only be derailed by a change in plans regarding the location of the center. Ultimately, the mosque and community center were indeed opened in 2011, only for the developer to petition in 2014 for a right to demolish and redevelop the property for a new Islamic museum on the same site.

Perhaps the most interesting feature of the Terry Jones episode (which ended when Jones unceremoniously announced that God had called upon him to change his mind) was how quickly this local incident became an international conflagration, with senior military and political figures warning of retaliation against U.S. troops stationed abroad and foreign leaders and diplomats calling for federal intervention. This explosion of interest may have been exacerbated by mainstream media, but it was almost certainly fanned by online communities and bloggers focusing a spotlight on what might otherwise have proved an obscure act. Such is the power of modern digital communications that words, sounds, and images collected in one place are instantaneously available to others across the street or around the world. In light of their continuing power to influence perception and value, religion and transcendent beliefs become foci for disagreement in a way that would have been impossible even a generation ago. As late as the 1980s, it was possible for a discrete request made to a senior newspaper or media editor to prevent knowledge of certain events from being released. In the past twenty years, our understanding of what "gate keepers" are has been radically transformed to the point where it is difficult even to identify any. In this age of the twenty-four-hour cable news cycle, fueled by leagues of i-Reporters and citizen journalists, we should only expect ever-deeper fault lines to appear and chasms to open in which faith is pitted against faith and religion against state.

This first section presents a collection of reports that illuminate not only the way in which such conflicts have unfolded, but also the general confusion, head scratching, and apparent bafflement that often accompanies them. Considering the scope of these articles, it is fair to say that many in the United States and elsewhere tend to esteem religion and transcendent phenomena without necessarily knowing a great deal about the historical and cultural foundations for any practice or institution in particular. Articles presented in this section all raise important questions concerning the status of religion and religious change in the early twenty-first century. What does religion mean for Americans and other Westerners living in a time of cultural and religious plurality? How does a person's age and life position affect adherence to religion? Is it possible to sustain spirituality and faith in the absence of institutional religion? Beyond the United States, articles on the acceptability of religious symbolism in Italian classrooms and the use of public transportation as a vehicle (so to speak) for debating religion in public, address a simmering tension in European society between defenders of civil libertinism and separation of church and state on one hand, and religious traditionalists on the other. As the European Union becomes progressively "de-churched," the presence of religious traditionalists of various stripes poses a challenge to those citizens seeking to root their European identities in Christianity—increasingly excluded from the public sphere and relegated to private life.

It is hoped that questions such as these will provide grist for lively classroom conversation and debate about where all things religious and supernatural stand in the uncharted waters of twenty-first-century America.

II

AMERICANS SWITCH FAITHS OFTEN

"Religion à la Carte" Is Pervasive, Sociology Professor Says

DAVID DUPREY

T he United States is a nation of religious drifters, with about half of adults switching faith affiliation at least once during their lives, according to a new survey.

The reasons behind the swap depend greatly on whether one grows up kneeling at Roman Catholic Mass, praying in a Protestant pew or occupied with nonreligious pursuits, according to a report issued Monday by the Pew Forum on Religion and Public Life.

While Catholics are more likely to leave the church because they stopped believing its teachings, many Protestants are driven to trade one Protestant denomination or affiliation for another because of changed life circumstances, the survey found.

The ranks of those unaffiliated with any religion, meanwhile, are growing not so much because of a lack of religious belief but because of disenchantment with religious leaders and institutions.

The report estimates that between 47 percent and 59 percent of U.S. adults have changed affiliation at least once. Most described just gradually drifting away from their childhood faith.

"This shows a sort of religion a la carte and how pervasive it is," said D. Michael Lindsay, a Rice University sociologist of religion. "In some ways, it's an indictment of organized Christianity. It suggests there's a big open door for newcomers, but a wide back door where people are leaving."

Religion-Swapping

The report, "Faith in Flux: Changes in Religious Affiliation in the U.S.," sought to answer questions about widespread religion-changing identified in a 2007 Pew survey of 35,000 Americans.

The new report, based on re-interviews with more than 2,800 people from the original survey, focuses on religious populations that showed a lot of movement: ex-Catholics, ex-Protestants, Protestants who have swapped denominational families within Protestantism and people raised unaffiliated who now belong to a faith.

The 2007 survey estimated that 44 percent of U.S. adults had left their childhood religious affiliation.

But the re-interviews found the extent of religion-swapping is likely much greater. The new survey revealed that one in six Americans who belong to their childhood faith are "reverts"—people who left the faith, only to return later.

Roughly two-thirds of those raised Catholic or Protestant who now claim no religious affiliation say they have changed faiths at least twice. Thirty-two percent of unaffiliated ex-Protestants said they've changed three times or more.

Age Is Another Factor

Age is another factor. Most people who left their childhood faith did so before turning 24, and a majority joined their current religion before 36.

"If people want to see a truly free market at work, they really should look at the U.S. religious marketplace," said Luis Lugo, director of the Pew Forum on Religion and Public Life.

Sixteen percent of U.S. adults identified as unaffiliated in the 2007 survey; 7 percent of Americans described being raised unaffiliated, suggesting that many Americans end up leaving their religion for none.

About half of those who have become unaffiliated cited a belief that religious people are hypocritical, judgmental or insincere. Large numbers said they think religious organizations focus too much on rules, or that religious leaders are too focused on money and power.

"Dissatisfied Customers"

John Green, a University of Akron political scientist and a senior fellow with the Pew Forum, classified most unaffiliated as "dissatisfied consumers." Only 4 percent identify as atheist or agnostic, and one-third say they just haven't found the right religion.

"A lot of the unaffiliated seem to be OK with religion in the abstract," Green said. "It's just the religion they were involved in bothered them or they disagreed with it."

The unaffiliated category is not just a destination. It's also a departure point: a slight majority of those raised unaffiliated eventually join a faith tradition.

Those who do cite several reasons: attraction of religious services and worship (74 percent), feeling unfulfilled spiritually (51 percent) or feeling called by God (55 percent).

The survey found that Catholicism has suffered the greatest net loss in all the religion switching. Nearly six in 10 former Catholics who are now unaffiliated say they left Catholicism due to dissatisfaction with Catholic teachings on abortion and homosexuality. About half cited concerns about Catholic teachings on birth control and roughly four in ten named unhappiness with Catholicism's treatment of women.

Staying in the Fold

Converts to evangelicalism were more likely to cite their belief that Catholicism didn't take the Bible literally enough, while mainline Protestants focused more on the treatment of women.

Fewer than three in 10 former Catholics cited the clergy sexual abuse scandal as a factor—a finding that Washington Archbishop Donald Wuerl cited as an example of the faith's resilience.

"Catholics can separate the sins and human failings of individuals from the substance of the faith," Wuerl said in a statement.

Wuerl noted a finding that getting teenagers to weekly Mass greatly improves their chances of staying in the fold; the same holds true for Protestant teens attending services.

The survey found that 15 percent of Americans were raised as Protestants but now belong to a different Protestant tradition than their upbringing. Nearly four in 10 cited a move to a new community, while one-third said they married someone from a different background.

||||||||||||||||||||||||||||||||||||||||||||||||||||||||||||||||

TEENS SERIOUS ABOUT RELIGION

MSNBC.COM

The majority of American teens believe in God and worship in conventional congregations, but their religious knowledge is remarkably shallow, and they have a tough time expressing the difference that faith makes in their lives, a new survey says.

Still, the notably comprehensive National Study of Youth and Religion concluded that "religion really does matter" to teens.

The research found that devout teens hold more traditional sexual and other values than their nonreligious counterparts and are better off in emotional health, academic success, community involvement, concern for others, trust of adults and avoidance of risky behavior.

The four-year effort was conducted by 133 researchers and consultants led by sociologist Christian Smith of the University of North Carolina at Chapel Hill. Smith reports the full results in the new book *Soul Searching: The Religious and Spiritual Lives of American Teenagers* (Oxford University Press), written with doctoral student Melinda Lundquist Denton. The book will be published next week.

Smith says the material "is not just about teenagers. It speaks more broadly about the direction of American religion."

Most Follow Parents' Path

The project involved a telephone survey of 3,370 randomly selected English- and Spanish-speaking Americans, ages 13–17, followed by face-to-face interviews with 267 of the respondents in 45 states. With ongoing funding from the Lilly Endowment, researchers will continue to track the same teens through 2007.

While America is becoming a more diverse nation, at least 80 percent of teens still identify as Protestant, Roman Catholic, Eastern Orthodox, Mormon or Jewish, with most teens adhering to their parents' faith tradition, the report said.

Substantial majorities said they:

- Were affiliated with a local congregation (82 percent).
- Had few or no doubts about their beliefs in the past year (80 percent).
- Felt "extremely," "very" or "somewhat" close to God (71 percent).
- Prayed alone a few times a week or more often (65 percent).
- "Definitely" believed in divine miracles from God (61 percent).

Fifty-two percent said they attended worship two to three times a month or more often.

On most of the measured criteria, Mormon youths—whose church runs daily high school religion classes—were the most engaged in practicing their faith, followed in order by evangelical Protestants, black Protestants, mainline Protestants, Catholics and Jews.

An entire chapter of the book examines Catholic youths, described as fairly weak "on most measures of religious faith, belief, experience and practice." The problem is attributed largely to ineffective youth programs and "the relative religious laxity of their parents."

Among Jews, only 44 percent believed in a personal God who is involved in peoples' lives today, and 34 percent said they never pray alone.

Future reports from the researchers will provide more detail on teens from specific religious denominations.

Meager, Nebulous ... Fallacious

Though the phone survey depicted broad affinity with religion, the face-to-face interviews found that many teens' religious knowledge was "meager, nebulous and often fallacious" and engagement with the substance of their traditions remarkably shallow. Most seemed hard put to express coherently their beliefs and what difference they make.

Many were so detached from the traditions of their faith, says the report, that they're virtually following a different creed in which an undemanding God exists mostly to solve problems and make people feel good. Truth in any absolute, theological sense, takes a back seat.

"God is something like a combination Divine Butler and Cosmic Therapist" who's on call as needed, Smith writes. He says the trend reflects tendencies among teens' Baby Boomer parents. The report speculates that poor educational and youth programs, and competition for teens' time from school, sports, friends and entertainment also are part of the picture.

In an interview, Smith—an Episcopal layman with children ages 13, 11 and six—said fellow parents should know that "teens are not from another planet. They're just people like everyone else. They're a lot more connected to the adult world, and listening to their parents, than people have any idea of."

No margin of error was released, though the response rate of 57 percent in the 2002–03 phone survey makes the results statistically significant, Smith said, with variations depending on the group being discussed.

III

EUROPEAN UNITY TESTED OVER CRUCIFIXES IN CLASSROOM

If European Court's Ruling Stands, Symbol Will Be Removed from Schools

VICTOR L. SIMPSON

An emotional debate over crucifixes in classrooms is opening a new crack in European unity.

It all started in a small town in northern Italy, where Finnish-born Soile Lautsi was so shocked by the sight of crosses above the blackboard in her children's public school classroom that she called a lawyer to see if she could get them removed.

Her case went all the way to Europe's highest court—and her victory has set up a major confrontation between traditional Catholic and Orthodox countries and nations in the north that observe a strict separation between church and state. Italy and more than a dozen other countries are fighting the European Court of Human Rights ruling, contending the crucifix is a symbol of the continent's historic and cultural roots.

"This is a great battle for the freedom and identity of our Christian values," said Italian Foreign Minister Franco Frattini.

The court case underlines how religious symbols are becoming a contentious issue in an increasingly multiethnic Europe.

French legislators begin debate next week on a draft law, vigorously championed by President Nicolas Sakorzy, that would forbid women from wearing face-covering Islamic veils anywhere in public. Belgium and Spain are considering similar laws.

In its Nov. 3 ruling, the European Court of Human Rights accepted Lautsi's contention that a crucifix could be disturbing to non-Christian pupils and said state-run schools must observe "confessional neutrality."

Rulings of the court are binding on the 47 members of the Council of Europe, Europe's chief human rights watchdog.

Crucifixes are on display in many public buildings in Italy, where the Vatican is located, and the Roman Catholic Church has encouraged support for keeping them. They will be taken down in schools, however, if the court ruling stands.

Despite the rhetoric, Italy has given no hint that the issue would be enough to compel it to quit the council, something no country has ever done.

Arguing the appeal Wednesday, New York University legal scholar Joseph Weiler stressed the importance of national symbols "around which society can coalesce."

"It would be strange (if Italy) had to abandon national symbols, and strip from its cultural identity any symbol which also had a religious significance," said Weiler, an Orthodox Jew who wore a yarmulke while addressing the 19-judge panel.

Taken to the extreme, Weiler elaborated in an interview with Italy's La Stampa newspaper, the case for secularism could endanger Britain's national anthem "God Save the Queen."

Simmering Debate

Lined up with Italy are such traditional Catholic bastions as Malta, San Marino and Lithuania. The Foreign Ministry of the late Pope John Paul II's Poland—where crucifixes are displayed in public schools and even in the hall of parliament—says the country "supports all actions that the government of Italy has taken before the Council of Europe."

The list also includes such heavily Orthodox Christian countries as Greece and Cyprus, as well as Russia, Ukraine and Bulgaria, which lived through religious persecution under communism.

"The support from so many other countries—we are talking here about a third of the membership of the Council of Europe—has given the case great political significance," said Gregor Puppinck, director of the European Center for Law and Justice, a Christian lobbying group.

A final ruling is not expected before fall. Lautsi filed the first complaint in 2002, and both her children are now in their early 20s.

The debate over the role religion should play on the largely secular continent has been simmering for more than a decade.

For years, Pope John Paul called on the European Union to include a reference to the continent's Judeo-Christian heritage in a new constitution, lecturing European leaders whenever they came to Rome. But France and other northern countries blocked such wording.

John Paul's successor, Pope Benedict XVI, urged Europeans to defend their continent's religious and cultural heritage just a week after the November verdict on crucifixes.

Benedict has held up the United States as an example, saying he admires "the American people's historic appreciation of the role of religion in shaping public discourse." The U.S. Supreme Court has ruled in favor of government displays of religious materials such as the Ten Commandments when their purpose was educational or historical rather than religious.

Critics Claim a Double Standard

Some Muslims in Europe see supporters of crucifixes in classrooms as applying a double standard to religious tolerance.

Said Bouamama, a Muslim sociologist and specialist in immigration questions in France, says the push by Italy and other nations "reflects a clear preference for Christianity, meaning that tolerance is only extended towards one religion and not for all."

Such a measure must be "either for everyone or for no one. If not, it will produce even greater division," said Bouamama, a researcher at a French institute that trains social workers.

France has western Europe's largest Muslim population, about 5 million, and largest Jewish population, about half a million. Its generally moderate Muslim community has shown itself reluctant to pursue court action in cases involving clothing issues, as when France barred Muslim headscarves from classrooms in 2004.

|||||||||||||||||||||||||||||||||||||||||||||||||||||||||||||||||||

IN FINAL INTERVIEW, CARDINAL SAYS CHURCH 200 YEARS OUT OF DATE

NAOMI O'LEARY

The former archbishop of Milan and papal candidate Cardinal Carlo Maria Martini said the Catholic Church was "200 years out of date" in his final interview before his death, published on Saturday.

Martini, once favored by Vatican progressives to succeed Pope John Paul II and a prominent voice in the church until his death at the age of 85 on Friday, gave a scathing portrayal of a pompous and bureaucratic church failing to move with the times.

"Our culture has aged, our churches are big and empty and the church bureaucracy rises up, our rituals and our cassocks are pompous," Martini said in the interview published in Italian daily Corriere della Sera.

"The Church must admit its mistakes and begin a radical change, starting from the pope and the bishops. The pedophilia scandals oblige us to take a journey of transformation," he said in the interview.

In the last decade the Church has been accused of failing to fully address a series of child abuse scandals which have undermined its status as a moral arbiter, though it has paid many millions in compensation settlements worldwide.

Martini, famous for comments that the use of condoms could be acceptable in some cases, told interviewers the Church should open up to new kinds of families or risk losing its flock.

"A woman is abandoned by her husband and finds a new companion to look after her and her children. A second love succeeds. If this family is discriminated against, not just the mother will be cut off but also her children."

In this way "the Church loses the future generation", Martini said in the interview, made a fortnight before he died. The Vatican opposes divorce and forbids contraception in favor of fidelity within marriage and abstinence without.

A liberal voice in the church, Martini's chances of becoming pope were damaged when he revealed he was suffering from a rare form of Parkinson's disease and he retired in 2002.

Pope John Paul II was instead succeeded in 2005 by Pope Benedict XVI, a hero of Catholic conservatives who is known by such critical epithets as "God's rottweiler" because of his stern stand on theological issues.

Martini's final message to Pope Benedict was to begin a shake up of the Catholic church without delay.

"The church is 200 years out of date. Why don't we rouse ourselves? Are we afraid?"

Martini was much loved and thousands paid their respects at his coffin in Milan cathedral on Saturday.

||||||||||||||||||||||||||||||||||||||||||||||||||||||||||||||

VATICAN OFFICIAL CALLS ATHIEST THEORIES "ABSURD"

MSNBC.COM

A Vatican cardinal said Tuesday that the Catholic Church does not stand in the way of scientific realities like evolution, though he described as "absurd" the atheist notion that evolution proves there is no God.

Cardinal William Levada, head of the Vatican's Congregation for the Doctrine of the Faith, reiterated church teaching about faith and science at the start of a Vatican-sponsored conference marking the 150th anniversary of Charles Darwin's *On the Origin of Species*.

Speaking on the sidelines of the conference, Levada said the Vatican believed there was a "wide spectrum of room" for belief in both the scientific basis for evolution and faith in God the creator.

"We believe that however creation has come about and evolved, ultimately God is the creator of all things," he said.

He said that while the Vatican did not exclude any area of science, it did reject as "absurd" the atheist notion of biologist and author Richard Dawkins and others that evolution proves there is no God.

"Of course we think that's absurd and not at all proven," he said. "But other than that … the Vatican has recognized that it doesn't stand in the way of scientific realities."

The Vatican under Pope Benedict XVI has been trying to stress its belief that there is no incompatibility between faith and reason, and the five-day conference at Rome's Pontifical Gregorian University is a key demonstration of its efforts to engage with the scientific community.

Intelligent Design?

Church teaching holds that Catholicism and evolutionary theory are not necessarily at odds. But the Vatican's position became somewhat confused in recent years, in part because of a 2005 New York Times op-ed piece written by a close Benedict collaborator, Austrian Cardinal Christoph Schoenborn.

In the piece, Schoenborn seemed to reject traditional church teaching and back intelligent design, the view that life is too complex to have developed through evolution alone, and that a higher power has had a hand in changes among species over time.

Vatican officials later made clear they did not believe intelligent design was science and that teaching it alongside evolutionary theory in school classrooms only created confusion.

The evolution conference will explore intelligent design later this week, although not as science or theology but as a cultural phenomenon.

In his remarks, Levada referred to both Dawkins and the debate over teaching creationism in schools in the United States. He declined to pinpoint the Vatican's views, saying merely: "The Vatican listens and learns."

ATHEIST CHURCH SPLIT

ARTICLE 6

Sunday Assembly and Godless Revival's "Denominational Chasm"

HUFFINGTONPOST.COM

T hough the Sunday Assembly "atheist church" was founded just last year by comedians Pippa Evans and Sanderson Jones, it expanded quickly from just one London congregation to 28 in cities around the world. Perhaps then, it isn't so surprising that its dynamism has now led to a schism within the newly minted group.

A blog post by Lee Moore, a founder of The Godless Revival, titled, "The Sunday Assembly has a Problem with Atheism," outlined the issues that led to the break.

He said that he initially volunteered with Sunday Assembly NYC after Sanderson Jones brought his movement to the United States, becoming an organizing member who helped determine the U.S. branch's future after Jones left. Moore explained, "A minority of organizers wished to make the event not a show but an actual church service and agreed with Jones about cutting out the word Atheist, not having speakers from the Atheist community, avoiding having an Atheist audience, and moving the show out of a bar setting to a more formal church-like setting."

CNN reports that Jones denied telling the NYC group to stop using the word "atheism," but acknowledged that he told them "not to cater solely to atheists." He also recommended choosing a more family-friendly venue rather than the dive bar where they originally gathered.

Moore alleged that after some successful events, a minority on the board which preferred not to use the word "atheist" resigned en-masse with Jones' blessing, "with the intent to turn the Sunday Assembly into something more like a Unitarian church service."

"What started out as a comedic Atheist church wants to turn itself into some sort of centralized humanist religion," he wrote, "with Sanderson Jones and Pippa Evans at the helm."

Moore didn't let his differences with Jones and Evans deter him from the overall benefit of a regular meeting for atheists, and has now founded The Godless Revival as an alternative to Sunday Assembly NYC. He announced in the blog post, "Michael Dorian, a former NYC SA board member and NY State Director for American Atheists, has teamed-up with Don Albert, another former board member and musical director for NYC SA, and myself to bring you something new. We have named this new endeavor The Godless Revival, and it will be the celebration of Atheism that you deserve."

Jones told CNN that the split was "very sad," but overall contributed to the vibrancy of the atheist community itself. He said, "Ultimately, it is for the benefit of the community. One day, I hope there will soon be communities for every different type of atheist, agnostic and humanist. We are only one flavor of ice cream, and one day we hope there'll be congregations for every godless palate."

II

CHRISTIANS COUNTER ATHEISTS—ON LONDON BUSES

As Anti-God Ad Campaign Ends, Religious Groups Prepare Rebuttals

AKIRA SUEMORI

Christians are soldiering on in the battle over God's existence by putting ads on London's famous red buses urging people to have faith.

The posters are a response to an atheist campaign that told people to stop worrying about religion because God probably doesn't exist.

The Christian Party has paid $22,000 to run ads declaring: "There definitely is a God. So join the Christian Party and enjoy your life," in red, pink and orange letters.

The ads will start appearing buses Monday, just as a monthlong campaign by atheists ends. In that campaign, atheists paid for bus ads saying there is probably no God, so "stop worrying and enjoy your life."

The atheist campaign, organized by the British Humanist Association and backed by Oxford University biologist and author Richard Dawkins, sparked a debate over religious—or anti-religious—messages in public spaces.

Ad Authority Wouldn't Intervene

More than 300 people complained to Britain's advertising watchdog, arguing the atheist ads were misleading and denigrated people's faith. Christian groups decided to respond after the Advertising Standards Authority dismissed the complaints.

"The atheist campaign has been something of a red rag to Christians and was begging for a response," said George Hargreaves, the head of the Christian Party, a religious group that fields candidates for elections to the European Parliament. "I got tired of seeing these messages on buses driving past my window and want to give people the chance to read something with hope."

Another Christian group has also joined the campaign, with a more confrontational message from Psalm 53:1, which reads: "The fool hath said in his heart, There is no God." That ad will run for two weeks.

And the Russian Orthodox Church has joined in with an ad reading: "There is a God, believe. Don't worry and enjoy your life."

Hanne Stinson, chief executive of the British Humanist Society, said the society supported the right of religious groups to post their messages but said the advertisements were "dogmatic and declaratory, leaving no room for reason and debate."

"Our ads were undogmatic and funny, with the addition of the 'probably' in line with the continuing openness of humanists to new evidence," she said in a statement on the British Humanist Association Web site.

|||||||||||||||||||||||||||||||||||||||||||||||||||||||||||||||||||

TRANSGENDER MORMONS STRUGGLE TO FEEL AT HOME, IN RELIGION

PEGGY FLETCHER STACK

Sixteen-year-old Grayson Moore had no label, only metaphors, to describe the disconnect he felt between his body and soul.

It was like car sickness, he said, when your eyes and inner ears disagree about whether you are moving.

"It makes you sick," Moore said, according to The Salt Lake Tribune (http://bit.ly/1EY7eWs). "That's the same with gender."

When Moore's mother gave her then-daughter a vocabulary for the feelings—"gender dysphoria" or transgender—there followed an immediate sense of relief and recognition.

And, he said, God confirmed that he was not just a tomboy. He was in the wrong body.

Such moments come in the life of all transgender persons—times when vague feelings of general discomfort with their identity crystallize into that realization.

Annabel Jensen was deciding whether to serve a Mormon mission. Sara Jade Woodhouse was married and had fathered a child.

In these three cases, their Mormonism—with its emphasis on the physical link between bodies and spirits and its insistence that gender is "eternal"—initially made it tougher to acknowledge what was happening inside of them.

Since switching genders (though none has had sex-reassignment surgery), all three said they have found psychological and theological peace, even divine approval, and a surprising welcome from their local LDS leaders and congregations.

They are among a growing but little understood minority in The Church of Jesus Christ of Latter-day Saints.

Transgender Mormons in Utah have formed a support group, march in gay pride parades—though most are not gay—and talk openly about their experiences. A weekly "Family Home Evening" group routinely draws about 30 participants along the Wasatch Front.

Efforts to bring awareness are crucial, they believe, because most members of the Utah-based faith know little or nothing about what it's like to be transgender. And many judge and reject transgender loved ones.

Even LDS apostle Dallin H. Oaks acknowledged recently that Mormon leaders "have not had so much experience with (transgender persons).... We have some unfinished business on that."

Still, the faith does have policies in place, saying elective sex-reassignment surgery "may be cause for formal church discipline," according to the church's Handbook.

In some Mormon missions, including Thailand, with its many transgender persons, missionaries ask would-be converts if they are in their "original gender."

An official LDS document, "The Family: A Proclamation to the World," written and approved by the faith's top leaders, states that "gender is an essential characteristic of individual premortal, mortal, and eternal identity and purpose."

"Because of this," church spokesman Eric Hawkins writes in an emailed statement, "the church does not baptize those who are planning transsexual operations. If a person has already had such an operation and wishes to join the church, they may be baptized only after an interview with the mission president and approval by the First Presidency.

"The church does not ordain transgender people to the priesthood or issue temple recommends to them," Hawkins adds. "Church leaders counsel already-baptized members against elective transsexual operations, and bishops may refer specific cases to the stake president for possible resolution at that level or by the First Presidency.

"We have faith that ultimately, the emotional pain that many of these people feel will be addressed by a loving God who understands each individual's circumstances and heart."

Hawkins declined to comment about the church standing and prohibitions for those who have had only hormone treatments.

Many active LDS transgender persons accept the church's statements about gender being an essential characteristic and are willing to live with some restrictions.

Still, despite how comfortable transgender Mormons are in their new skin, the LDS Church is a very gendered place—men go to priesthood meetings, women to Relief

Society; men officiate at rituals and general meetings, women lead auxiliaries; men sit on one side in the temple, women, generally, on the other—and that complicates their lives inside the faith.

Growing up in Davis County—or "Mormonopolis," as Moore calls it—the young Latter-day Saint girl named Grace had severe panic attacks beginning in late elementary school and continuing through junior high. By high school, says the 22-year-old math major at the University of Utah, his distress—including physical symptoms such as nausea—was so extreme he hardly could function.

Moore's mother, Neca Allgood, took him to various doctors but no one could diagnose his problems.

Trained as a molecular biologist and a scientist by instinct, Allgood had a suspicion that her daughter might have "gender dysphoria."

When Allgood asked Moore if he was a girl in his body but a boy in his brain, the young man simply said, "not just my brain—in my soul."

With that recognition, Moore's life, at last, made sense to him.

"There's a word for it," he remembers thinking, "I'm not crazy."

That night, Grace Moore knelt in prayer, asking God, "Am I your son?"

He said he got a powerful spiritual affirmation that he was, indeed, a boy and that "it was going to be OK."

His mother essentially received the same message.

"The answer to my prayers was to love him and help him live as a boy," she said. "It increased my testimony and understanding of the Holy Spirit."

Mother and son talked it over and decided he needed to transition quickly.

During six weeks of his junior year in high school, Grace became Grayson, tossed out all the girl clothes, and began identifying as male.

Allgood was supportive, but worried about her son's safety.

"There was a bigger risk in not transitioning," he said. "Living that lie was killing me."

When he prayed about whether to begin taking testosterone treatment, he says the answer was to "wait," which he did. By college, however, he says he got the divine go-ahead and has seen a change as his body has become more male.

Moore has not yet had surgery but doesn't rule it out.

He attends an LDS singles ward, where he has the full support of his Mormon bishop. He goes to the male-only priesthood meetings but hasn't been ordained—and, under current church policy, won't be.

He's still listed as a female on LDS membership rolls.

Discussion Questions

1. How would you characterize modern US attitudes toward religion and religious organizations? In what ways do Americans change their religious beliefs and practices throughout life?
2. In what ways has the relationship between church and state been a troubled one in both the United States and Europe?
3. Discuss Christian responses to atheism, both from the point of view of church clergy and the rank-and-file faithful. Which elements stand out as most important to this dispute?
4. What do you think disputes and controversies within the LDS Church (Mormons) mean for the future of faith?

Further Readings

1. John R. Bowen. *Why the French Don't Like Headscarves: Islam, the State, and Public Space.* Princeton University Press, 2008.
   An important anthropological work that examines the current resonance of Muslim headscarves as a symbol of malaise among the broader French public. Bowen shows how legal proscriptions are boundaries erected in response to widely held public perceptions about the meaning of "Frenchness" and its antithesis in the non-French, non-Christian populations in urban France.
2. Chester Gillis. *Roman Catholicism in America.* New York: Columbia University Press, 2000.
   Gillis provides a compelling overview of the history of Catholicism in the United States, and shows how late-twentieth-century American Catholics incorporate (and sometimes avoid incorporating) traditional perspectives, values, and activities into their culture of faith.
3. Melvyn Hammarberg. *The Mormon Quest for Glory: The Religious World of the Latter-Day Saints.* Oxford University Press, 2013.

This rich anthropological analysis of the contemporary LDS Church offers perhaps the most in-depth, up-to-date look at the meaning of belief, ritual, and history among Mormons. Hammarberg's meticulous ethnography shows how everyday life and identity are organized, integrated, and infused with both social and spiritual value.

4. John T. S. Madeley and Zsolt Enyedi, eds. *Church and State in Contemporary Europe: The Chimera of Neutrality*. Abingdon, UK: Routledge, 2003.

This edited, cross-disciplinary volume contains essays by a number of scholars who explore various aspects of the current relations between church and state in various European regions, including Ireland, Italy, Spain, Poland, Hungary, Greece, Germany, and the Czech Republic.

5. Janet Reitman. *Inside Scientology: The Story of America's Most Secretive Religion*. New York: Houghton Mifflin, 2011.

In this critically acclaimed work of investigative journalism, Reitman explores the details of L. Ron Hubbard's biography and the history and inner workings of the Church of Scientology as few have done before. Her exposé is among the best examinations of a new religious movement published to date.

6. Mitchell Stephens. *Imagine There's No Heaven: How Atheism Helped Create the Modern World*. New York: St. Martin's Press, 2014.

This well-researched journalistic account documents the emergence and influence of atheistic philosophies from antiquity through the twenty-first century. In particular, he shows how advances in human knowledge and ethical behavior (such as the Enlightenment, Scientific Revolution, abolitionism, and organized labor) have grown in part out of deep questioning of such concepts as God and the divine right of kings.

7. David W. Stowe. *No Sympathy for the Devil: Christian Pop Music and the Transformation of American Evangelicalism*. Chapel Hill: University of North Carolina Press, 2011.

   Stowe explores the fast-growing world of Christian popular music in the United States, particularly with respect to the ways it has been influenced by mainstream rock music. The blossoming and popularity of Christian music reveals ways in which young people in evangelical churches respond to new social and technological circumstances in the twenty-first century, and avoid the various social stigmas attached by millennials and others to traditional evangelical religion.

8. James R. Lewis and Jesper Aa. Petersen, eds. *Controversial New Religions*, Second Edition. Oxford University Press, 2014.

   A wide-ranging sourcebook for readings on new, occult, unconventional, and controversial religions. Readings span a variety of categories of religious movements, from UFO and New Age religions to Eastern spiritualities and Western fundamentalisms.

TRANSCENDING SCIENCE

SECTION TWO
INTRODUCTION

One of the most polarizing cultural debates to exist in American society has involved those who see (rightly or wrongly) an unbridgeable gulf between science and religion. More specifically, the war of words and sometimes litigation between champions of evolutionary biology and theoretical physics, on one hand, and Christian intelligent design (a.k.a. creation science) on the other. The shorthand for such disputes, however—science versus religion—is misleading. While the vast majority of scientists are committed to what they do and the basic principles underlying their fields, most do not treat their work and methods as a religious system that provides such things as a theory of social relationships, ethics, and ultimate explanation of why things happen. As many have observed, scientists tend to be much better at and oriented toward explaining *how* things happen ... not *why*. Keeping this in mind, an unfortunate consequence of twentieth- and twenty-first-century debates is that they have often (but not always) involved people talking past one another on issues of central importance to all human beings.

Despite the claims of many, it is difficult to distill science and religion into an easy binary. From the early twentieth century, religious traditionalists have struggled against their understanding of a secular modernity that embraced godlessness through a disenchanted vision of the universe and, especially, the creation and biological development of human beings. While religious scholars and many people of faith have argued vigorously that no such bifurcation exists and that (to quote Pope John Paul II) "truth cannot contradict truth," Christian fundamentalists have succeeded in planting the idea of an intrinsic opposition in many layers of public discourse. In the age of televangelism and (with the Internet) post-televangelism, opponents of science education in the public school system have refined their tactics, becoming ever craftier in how they frame their message. From the 1980s, old-style creationism (in which the first chapters of Genesis were in effect the textbook for understanding human origins) has been restyled as intelligent design, and instead of rejecting scientific methods outright, more recent generations of fundamentalists have proposed that they offer a scientific alternative to Darwinian evolutionary theory. In general terms, this perspective holds that a species as gifted and complex as humans could hardly be random—the accidental product of genetic mutations interacting with an indifferent ecology. Instead, they propose that human complexity and dominance furnish evidence that we are central to God's plan for the world, and that such is borne out in both the archaeological and paleoanthropological records. Furthermore, such arguments are not confined to arguing the distant past, as the future too seems a bone of contention. As one of the readings in section two demonstrates, for many U.S. Christians "end of the world" prophecies provide an imperfect road map to a perfect future—by way of an apocalyptic event from which only the godly will emerge unscathed. However comforting such claims may prove for many, they have been roundly dismissed in all quarters of the academic and research establishments as ideologically charged anti-science that neither collects nor analyzes data in a way that would be recognized as legitimate by trained professionals.

Another, more subtle way in which science has engaged the broader culture in the media is by way of research, writing, and spectacle (mostly in the form of television reality series) that claim to objectively investigate whether transcendent beings such as ghosts really exist or whether the fictional physiology behind the apocalyptic, flesh-eating zombie is based on real science. Not surprisingly, the kind of answers such sources provide are dependent on whether the researcher(s) are motivated by the entertainment value and "sponsored content" of such narratives or not. In this way, two of the articles in this section are representative of this tension. In contrast to popular media sources that tickle the imagination with the possibility that such creatures exist, have been seen, and are (perhaps) the object of official cover ups of one kind or another, articles on ghost sightings and zombie neurology tend to bring us all back down to earth—albeit in an entertaining fashion. So, for instance, the likely culprits behind many ghostly encounters (at least from the point of view of brain chemistry) are things like carbon monoxide poisoning and hallucination-generating ergot fungus (the latter, produced by rye grain, has also been speculated about in the context of symptoms of 1692 witchcraft at Salem—see section five). As for zombies, it turns out that undead cannibals are a useful teaching tool: as a concept, they provide a point of departure for discussion of how the brain works, as well as for modeling the origins and spread of infectious disease, pandemics, and the sensitive medical issues surrounding end-of-life decision making. That is, in an age when physiological and even sensitive brain activity can be discerned in the near dead, how does one determine when death truly occurs?

II

GOD AND SCIENCE

An Inner Conflict

ROBIN LLOYD

G od and science are inherently at odds, or so goes the story with roots that reach back nearly 400 years to the Inquisition's trial of Galileo on suspicion of heresy.

The ongoing effort of U.S. creationists to inject doubt about evolution into science classrooms in public schools is an example of that conflict, not to mention the polarizing arguments over the decades offered by numerous members of the clergy, politicians, and some atheist scientists and scholars including Richard Dawkins.

Now a new study suggests our minds are conflicted, making it so we have trouble reconciling science and God because we unconsciously see these concepts as fundamentally opposed, at least when both are used to explain the beginning of life and the universe.

But what is the source of this seeming "irreconcilable difference"—are we hard-wired for it, or is it tenacious cultural baggage?

The Experiments

Experiments headed up by psychologist Jesse Preston of the University of Illinois at Urbana-Champaign and her colleague Nicholas Epley of the University of Chicago provide some data to support the argument that the conflict is inherent, or hard-wired. They found that subjects apparently cannot easily give positive evaluations to both God and science as explanations for big questions, such as the origin of life and the universe, at the same time.

In one experiment, 129 volunteers, mostly undergrads, read short summaries of the Big Bang theory and the Primordial Soup Hypothesis, a scientific theory of the origin of life.

Half of the group then read a statement explaining that the theories were strong and supported by the data. The other half read that the theories "raised more questions than they answered." All of the subjects then completed a computer task where they were required to categorize various words as positive or negative.

During the task, the word "science" or "God" or a neutral control word was flashed on the screen before each positive/negative word. For instance, right before the word "awful" appeared, either the word "God" or "science" was flashed on the screen for 15 milliseconds—too brief to be seen but it registers unconsciously.

This is a standard experimental psychology approach designed to measure latent, or automatic, attitudes toward (or evaluations of) the priming word—in this case, God or science. Faster response times mean a closer association between two concepts, for example "science" and "great."

Preston and Epley found that subjects who read the statement in support of the scientific theories responded more quickly to positive words appearing just after the word "science" than those who had read statements critical of the scientific theories. Similarly, those who read the statement suggesting that the scientific theories were weak were slower than the other group (who read the theory-supportive statement) to identify negative words that appeared after they were primed with the word "God."

The results are detailed in the January issue of the *Journal of Experimental Social Psychology*. Financial support for the study was received from the National Science Foundation and the Social Sciences and Humanities Research Council of Canada.

Preston says her research shows that a dual belief system, for instance the idea that evolution explains biology but God set the process in motion, does not exist in our brains.

"We can only believe in one explanation at a time," she told *LiveScience*. "So although people can report explicitly, 'Look, I've been a Christian all my life, and yes, I also believe in science and I am a practicing chemist,' the question is, are these people really reconciling belief in God and science, or are they just believing in one thing at a time?"

When it comes to the ultimate questions, it's really just one thing at a time, Preston says. People rarely think about these problems, however, so most people live their lives without paying much attention to how the universe started or how life began, Preston said.

Behind the Findings

However, Hampshire College science historian Salman Hameed says Preston and Epley's framing of the issues and interpretation of their findings are bound up in a particular view of science and religion known as the "conflict thesis." Yes, sometimes particular scientific and religious claims conflict, but there are numerous examples of individuals, such as Isaac Newton, who saw no inherent conflict between their scientific and religious convictions, Hameed said.

The experiment's results actually may reveal cultural forces—a specific way of thinking about science and religion—dating back to the 19th century, Hameed said, and these have shaped people's thinking about science and religion.

"If society has been primed that science and religion have been in conflict, and that is the dominant narrative, then maybe all we are seeing is the effect of that priming, rather than the actual conflict," Hameed said. Society and journalists like conflict stories because they grab attention, but science and religion interactions are more complex and defy over-simplistic oppositional categories, he said.

Preston agrees that there is a cultural opposition that we are all aware of, which may be a background context for her experiments, but she said religion and science have grown apart in the last few centuries because science developed theories that are inconsistent with doctrine.

"To the extent that culture is the culmination of history—all our ideas, knowledge, and traditions—the opposition that grew between religion and science is a part of our culture," Preston said. "But it is part of the culture because the contradictions are well known, and become part of our knowledge structure. The concept of zero as a number is also part of our culture, for example. The cultural opposition we see between religion and science is not a superficial opposition like dog lovers vs. cat lovers."

The History of the Conflict

Some historians trace the idea that science and religion are in conflict back to Cornell University's Andrew White and New York University's John William Draper, proponents of the professionalization of science who wrote books in the mid-1800s that claimed there was an inherent conflict between science and religion, citing the Galileo affair as the classic case.

The affair led to the astronomer's house arrest on suspicion of heresy (not heresy itself), starting in 1633 until his death in 1642. Galileo argued that the Earth revolved around the sun, based in part on his telescope observations, counter to Church teaching that the Earth was the center of the universe.

But science historians, including John Hedley Brooke, have questioned the conflict thesis, and others have poked big holes in simplistic interpretations of the Galileo story. For instance, some historians point out that Galileo, a practicing Catholic, didn't want to oppose the Church, but rather to update its views and prevent it from losing ground to Protestant scholars. Also, the Church ultimately sentenced Galileo, who had many political enemies in the church, on a technicality.

Ultimately, Galileo has been mostly redeemed, thanks to the ongoing efforts of scientists and, in the end, some clergy.

The International Year of Astronomy kicked off this month as a year-long celebration of astronomy timed to coincide, in part, with the 400th anniversary of the first recorded observations made by Galileo with a telescope.

In 2000, Pope John Paul II issued a formal apology for Church errors during the past 2,000 years, including the trial of Galileo.

And in May of this year, according to the Associated Press, some Vatican officials will attend an international conference on the Galileo affair.

||||||||||||||||||||||||||||||||||||||||||||||||||||||||||||

TELEVANGELIST WARNS OF EVOLUTION DOOMSDAY

Pat Robertson Says a Vote Against Intelligent
Design Is a Vote Against God

INFORMATION LIBERATION

C onservative Christian televangelist Pat Robertson told citizens of a Pennsylvania town that they had rejected God by voting their school board out of office for supporting "intelligent design" and warned them Thursday not to be surprised if disaster struck.

Robertson, a former Republican presidential candidate and founder of the influential conservative Christian Broadcasting Network and Christian Coalition, has a long record of similar apocalyptic warnings and provocative statements.

Last summer, he hit the headlines by calling for the assassination of leftist Venezuelan President Hugo Chavez, one of President Bush's most vocal international critics.

"I'd like to say to the good citizens of Dover: if there is a disaster in your area, don't turn to God, you just rejected him from your city," Robertson said on his daily television show broadcast from Virginia, "The 700 Club."

"And don't wonder why he hasn't helped you when problems begin, if they begin. I'm not saying they will, but if they do, just remember, you just voted God out of your city. And if that's the case, don't ask for his help because he might not be there," he said.

The 700 Club claims a daily audience of around 1 million. It is also broadcast around the world, translated into more than 70 languages. (People for the American Way provided a video file of the 700 Club statement.)

In voting Tuesday, all eight school board members up for re-election in Dover, Pa., lost their seats after trying to introduce "intelligent design" to high school science students as an alternative to the theory of evolution.

Adherents of intelligent design argue that certain forms in nature are so complex that they are best seen as the handiwork of a designer rather than the result of natural selection. Opponents say it is the latest attempt by conservatives to introduce religion into the school science curriculum.

The Dover case sparked a trial in federal court that gained nationwide attention after the school board was sued by parents backed by the American Civil Liberties Union. The board ordered schools to read students a short statement in biology classes informing them that the theory of evolution is not established fact and that gaps exist in it.

The statement mentioned intelligent design as an alternate theory and referred students to a book that explained the theory further. A decision in the case is expected before the end of the year.

In 1998, Robertson warned the city of Orlando, Fla., that it risked hurricanes, earthquakes and terrorist bombs after it allowed homosexual organizations to put up rainbow flags in support of sexual diversity.

IIIIIIIIIIIIIIIIIIIIIIIIIIIIIIIIIIIIIIIIIIIIIIIIIIIIIIIIIIIIIIIII

GHOST SIGHTINGS COULD JUST BE HALLUCINATIONS CAUSED BY MOLD, SAY RESEARCHERS

ROBYN PENNACCHIA

Researchers at Clarkson University in Potsdam, NY are investigating the possibility that "ghost sightings" and "haunted houses" may not be evidence of an afterlife, as much as they are hallucinations produced by toxic mold.

The fact is, most of these "hauntings" occur in places with poor air quality, and there are molds, like rye ergot fungus, that are known to cause psychosis in humans. This isn't exactly unprecedented, as there have been cases where people thought they were being "haunted" who turned out to be suffering from carbon monoxide poisoning and other things like that.

Via Clarkson University:

> "Hauntings are very widely reported phenomena that are not well-researched," he said. "They are often reported in older-built structures that may also suffer poor air quality. Similarly, some people have reported depression, anxiety and other effects from exposure to biological pollutants in indoor air. We are trying to determine whether some reported hauntings may be linked to specific pollutants found in indoor air."

> Rogers is working with a group of undergraduate students to measure air quality in several reportedly haunted places around the North Country, including the Frederic Remington

Art Museum in Ogdensburg, N.Y. The team will gather data at several locations throughout the spring and summer and will publish their results at the end of the study.

By comparing these samples to samples from places with no reported haunt- ings, the researchers hope to identify factors unique to the haunted locations. They are looking for commonalities in the mold microbiome in the places believed to be haunted compared to the controls, as well as analyzing the types of toxic molds that may cause psychological effects in humans.

I am actually really grateful to these researchers. For years, I have found myself in an incredibly awkward conversational bind when it comes to ghosts and the fact that I don't believe in them, that goes a little something like this:

Me: I don't believe in ghosts.

Friend: Oh, ghosts are real. I have totally seen ghosts. Many ghosts. Let me tell you the story of a ghost I saw one time.

Me: That's cool, I just don't believe in them. I am 100% sure that ghosts are not a real thing.

Friend: ARE YOU CALLING ME A LIAR?

And really. There is no graceful exit from that conversation. There just isn't. Either I lie and say I've been convinced, bullshit and say "Oh, who can really know anything. Maybe I'm wrong!" or I say "Yes, I think you're a liar" or "I believe that you think you saw a ghost" which is a lot like telling someone you think they are nuts. There is basically no way to say you don't believe in ghosts without suggesting that some people are liars. Which is mean, and I don't like being mean!

But now I can say "well, some scientists suspect that ghost sightings may be caused by hallucinogens in mold" which I think is way less awkward than any of the other responses I have come up with so far.

||||||||||||||||||||||||||||||||||||||||||||||||||||||||||||

INSIDE ZOMBIE BRAINS

Sci-Fi Teaches Sciences

ELIZABETH LANDAU

An airborne virus is rapidly turning people into zombies. Two-thirds of humanity has been wiped out. Scientists desperately look for a cure, even as their own brains deteriorate and the disease robs them of what we consider life.

Relax, it's only fiction—at least, for now. This apocalyptic scenario frames the new novel "The Zombie Autopsies" by Dr. Steven Schlozman, a child psychiatrist who holds positions at Harvard Medical School and the Massachusetts General Hospital/McLean Program in Child Psychiatry.

You might not expect someone with those credentials to take zombies seriously, but it turns out the undead are a great way to explore real-world health issues: why certain nasty diseases can destroy the brain, how global pandemics create chaos and fear, and what should be done about people infected with a highly contagious and incurable lethal illness.

"One of the things zombie novels do is they bring up all these existential concerns that happen in medicine all the time: How do you define what's alive?" says Schlozman, who has been known to bounce between zombie fan conventions and academic meetings.

"When is it appropriate to say someone's 'as-good-as-dead,' which is an awful, difficult decision?"

What a Zombie Virus Would Do to the Brain

So maybe you've seen "Night of the Living Dead," read "World War Z," or can't wait for the return of the AMC show "The Walking Dead," but you probably don't know what differentiates the brains of humans and zombies.

First things first: How does the zombie disease infect its victims? Many stories in the genre talk about biting, but Schlozman's novel imagines a deliberately engineered virus whose particles can travel in the air and remain potent enough to jump from one person to another in a single sneeze.

Now, then, to the brain-eating. The zombie virus as Schlozman describes it basically gnaws the brain down to the amygdala, an almond-shaped structure responsible for the "fight or flight" response. The zombies always respond by fighting because another critical part of the brain, the ventromedial hypothalamus, which tells you when you've eaten enough, is broken.

The brain's frontal lobes, responsible for problem-solving, are devoured by the virus, so zombies can't make complex decisions. Impairment in the cerebellum means they can't walk well, either. Also, these humanoids have an unexplained predilection for eating human flesh.

"The zombies in this book are stumbling, shambling, hungry as hell," Schlozman said. "Basically they're like drunk crocodiles; they're not smart, they don't know who you are or what you are."

How a Zombie Virus Would Be Made

So the bloodthirsty undead wander (or crawl) around spreading a lethal illness ominously called ataxic neurodegenerative satiety deficiency syndrome, or ANSD, for short.

"When something really terrifying comes along, especially in medicine or that has a medical feel to it, we always give it initials. That's the way we distance ourselves from it," Schlozman said.

The virus has several brain-destroying components, one of which is a "prion," meaning a protein like the one that causes mad cow disease. In real life, prions twist when they are in an acidic environment and become dangerous, Schlozman said. How our own environment has changed to make prions infectious—getting from the soil to the cows in mad cow disease, for instance—is still a mystery.

Now here's something to send chills up your spine: In Schlozman's world, airborne prions can be infectious, meaning mad cow disease and similar nervous-system destroyers could theoretically spread just like the flu. Swiss and German researchers recently found that mice that had only one minute of exposure to aerosols containing prions died of mad cow disease, as reported in the journal PLoS Pathogens. A follow-up described in Journal of the American Medical Association showed the same for a related disease that's only found in animals called scrapie. Of course, these are mice in artificially controlled conditions in a laboratory, and humans do not exhale prions, but it could have implications for safety practices nonetheless.

Like mad cow disease, the zombie disease Schlozman describes also progresses in acidic environments. In the book, a major corporation doles out implantable meters that infuse the body with chemicals to artificially lower acidity when it gets too high. But, sadly, when acidity is too low, that also induces symptoms that mimic the zombie virus, so it's not a longterm solution. Everyone who gets exposed eventually succumbs, Schlozman said.

As for the unknown component of the zombie disease that would help slowly zombifying researchers in their quest for a cure, that's up for the reader to figure out—and the clues are all in the book, Schlozman said.

How We'd Fight Back

You can't ethically round up fellow survivors to kick some zombie butt unless the undead have technically died. And in Schlozman's book, a group of religious leaders get together and decide that when people reach stage four of the disease, they are basically dead. That, of course, permits zombie "deanimation," or killing.

And how do you kill a zombie? Much of zombie fiction knocks out zombies through shots to the head. That, Schlozman said, is because the brain stem governs the most basic functioning: breathing and heartbeat.

A zombie-apocalypse disease like the one he describes probably wouldn't evolve on its own in the real world, he said.

But, as we've seen, individual symptoms of zombies do correspond to real ailments. And if they all came together, the disease would be creepily efficient at claiming bodies, Schlozman said.

Bad news, folks: Even if people contracted a zombie virus through bites, the odds of our survival aren't great.

A mathematician at the University of Ottawa named Robert Smith? (who uses the question mark to distinguish himself from other Robert Smiths, of course), has calculated that if one zombie were introduced to a city of 500,000 people, after about seven days, every human would either be dead or a zombie.

"We're in big, big trouble if this ever happens," Smith? said. "We can kill the zombies a bit, but we're not very good at killing zombies fundamentally. What tends to happen is:

The zombies just win, and the more they win, the more they keep winning" because the disease spreads so rapidly.

The best solution is a strategic attack, rather than an "every man for himself" defense scenario, he said. It would take knowledge and intelligence, neither of which zombies have, to prevail.

Why Study Zombies?

In his day job, Smith? models how real infectious diseases spread. But he's already reaped benefits from his work on zombies. For instance, while many mathematical models only deal with one complicated aspect of a situation at a time, he tackled two—zombie infection and zombie-killing—when it came to speculating about outbreaks.

When it came time for modeling of real-world human papillomavirus (HPV), then, Smith? felt equipped to handle many facets of it at the same time, such as heterosexual and homosexual transmission of HPV.

"Knowing what we knew from zombies allowed us to actually take on these more complicated models without fear," he said.

Studying zombies is also a great way to get young people excited about science. Smith?, who was on a zombie-science panel with Schlozman through the National Academy of Sciences' Science and Entertainment Exchange in 2009, has also seen math-phobic people get interested in mathematics by reading about his work with zombies.

"There are insights that we gain from the movies, and from fiction, from fun popular culture stuff, that actually can really help us think about the way that science works, and also the way science is communicated," he said.

And as to why people like reading about zombies and watching zombies so much, Schlozman points to the impersonal nature of things in our society, from waiting in line in the DMV to being placed on hold on a call with a health insurance company.

Think about all the situations in daily life where you sense a general lack of respect for humanity, and zombies make a little more sense.

"The zombies themselves represent a kind of commentary on modernity," Schlozman says. "We're increasingly disconnected. That might be the current appeal."

Discussion Questions

1. What is the dual belief system, and how does it allow us to reconcile acceptance of science with belief in God?
2. What factors lead some U.S. evangelicals to imagine a global doomsday is imminent? Do these beliefs have consequences for US society more generally? Why? Why not?
3. What does research on the biochemistry of hallucinogenic experience tell us about beliefs in the transcendent? Do you think such research will affect how people think about such phenomena as ghosts? Why or why not?
4. How is the fictional idea of the zombie being used to inform modern scientific thought and research? Based on the article, what is the likelihood that "real" zombies could be created?

Further Readings

1. Randall Balmer. *Mine Eyes Have Seen the Glory: A Journey into the Evangelical Subculture in America*, 25th Anniversary Edition. Oxford University Press, 2014.
   This updated edition of a classic work delves into the multi-faceted world of American evangelicalism from the perspective of an historian. Balmer's book was the basis for an acclaimed PBS documentary, and explores such social microcosms as Bible Camp, the world of Christian booksellers, charismatic/revivalist meetings, and urban "crusades" among various subsets of U.S. believers (including Latinos and Native Americans).
2. Ian G. Barbour. *When Science Meets Religion: Enemies, Strangers, or Partners?* New York: HarperCollins Books, 2000.
   An excellent and accessible study of the relations among theology and religious ideology, and scientific perspectives and methods.

Barbour places special emphasis on the cosmos, biological evolution, and neurobiology. Throughout, he attempts to address important questions (such as where the universe and humanity come from) from the point of view of how to advance dialogue on all sides of these often fraught debates.

3. Alister E. McGrath. *Science and Religion: A New Introduction*, Second Edition. Chichester, UK: Wiley-Blackwell, 2009.

   A concise introduction to the history and character of debate between the worlds of the natural sciences and (mainly Christian) religion. McGrath, a biochemist and theologian, is well positioned to outline the main contours of various controversies, both historical and current: from Copernicus and Darwin to the "selfish gene" and evolutionary psychology.

4. Bertrand Russell. *Religion and Science.* Oxford University Press, 1997.

   In this book, Russell—an acclaimed philosopher and mathematician—provides a lucid overview of the relationships and tensions between science and religion over the last several centuries. This work will be of special interest to anyone wanting to compare episodes from early modernity (for instance the Copernican and Scientific Revolutions) to current debates concerning evolutionary theory and bioethics.

5. Daniel Wojcik. *The End of the World as We Know It: Faith, Fatalism, and Apocalypse in America.* NYU Press, 1999.

   Wojcik offers an engaging study of various doomsday and apocalyptic movements heading into the new millennium. In particular, he explores the history of a peculiar American fascination with end times, and provides cultural context to the many predictions of an imminent demise and possible rebirth to human civilization. Specific foci for investigation include nuclear catastrophe, religious apocalypse, and extraterrestrial invasion.

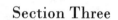

Section Three

MAGICAL
CULTURE

In the United States and around the world, magic has long been a term that evokes the entwined ideas of mystery and largely unseen power. Nevertheless, there is a fair amount of ambiguity surrounding the word as used in everyday speech, mostly because it is so semantically flexible; one can refer to the magic of the atmosphere of Disneyland or to the magic of an illusionist showman in Las Vegas; the magic of the *Harry Potter* novels or the magic of a first kiss. Routinely, we apply the word in a somewhat careless or even sarcastic way, to denote things or events that are too difficult or time consuming to explain systematically or rigorously. (I ask, "How did he get 99% on his calculus exam?" You respond, "Magic ... how else?") So, given this eclectic variety of uses, is it even possible or even desirable to settle on a fixed definition?

Traditionally, anthropologists have use the term magic to refer to the manipulation of transcendent power by a human agent, through the use of symbols and generally in the interests of achieving some real-world objective or practical change. This definition is both valuable and inadequate.

It is valuable, first, because it identifies a type of reasoning that can be mapped out in time and space across all human societies. There has never been a human society in which some symbolic thought and activity has not been put towards some practical achievement. This is true whether we are talking about fixing cars, filling cavities, or assuaging spirits whose help we need to "make things right." In each of these examples, magic involves a body of specialized technical knowledge and ability in the hands of an accredited professional who achieves a powerful result, even while the details of his or her action are invisible to untrained eyes. Of course, people will disagree as to whether the activities of neurosurgeons are as symbolic in character as those of traditional shamans and priests, but there is no doubt that medical doctors, too, wield symbolically powerful objects (stethoscopes, lab coats, scalpels, et cetera) that together paint a portrait of authority in the minds of the untrained. In this way, this idea that magic and magicians are universal and even archetypal is appealing for comparative analysis of how social institutions function to bestow meaning and order on a largely uncontrollable universe.

On the flip side of this coin (flipping coins, incidentally, is a mundane act of magical divination—fortune telling—if ever there was one), the term magic so defined is wholly inadequate for a more perceptive theory of human action, meaning, and motivation. This is because even the idea of magic (let alone the term) is, to use an anthropological phrase, "culture bound." This means that the term carries with it the historical baggage of many hidden assumptions that are difficult to purge in the first place, and nearly impossible in the second if we grant the term universal status as a natural "fact" of human life and culture.

To cite one well-worn example, the logic behind casual usage of the word magic, suggested above, tends to disguise an older, less frivolous application of the term to the religious traditions of non-Europeans, whose rituals seemed exotic, frightening, superstitious, and bizarre. An appropriate modern response to this ethnocentric assertion might be to observe that one person's religion is another person's magic and vice versa. In other words, my beliefs and practices are quite obviously right, logical, and compelling ,while yours are quite obviously incorrect, illogical, and repulsive. Clearly, religious beliefs and activities that are foreign to our own experience often seem illogical or even frightening. This was perhaps most especially true during the era of European discovery and colonization of the non-Western world (sixteenth to early-twentieth centuries) when most Europeans believed Christianity, science, and Western ways of understanding the world generally were self-evidently superior to the "primitive" practices of Native Americans, Africans, and other indigenous peoples around the globe.

And yet, to a degree that should make us all a bit uncomfortable, such assumptions and the language in which they are embedded (most especially in the words magic and witchcraft) persist into the twenty-first century—albeit in a more innocuous way than at the height of the colonial era. Consider the innocent entertainment value of the Harry Potter and Middle-Earth sagas by J.K. Rowling and J.R.R. Tolkien, respectively. On the page, both universes are unbridled, sprawling masterpieces of creative ingenuity. Since their commercial popularization as novels, both worlds have found even wider audiences via theatrical films that feature the latest optical effects bring to life a host of magical events, characters, and creatures. At least superficially, most of us would agree that such fantasy tales are fiction and, hence, at root unreal—created for the purposes of pure escapism from everyday routines and drudgery. The same might be said of a wide variety of television series grounded in the theme of magical powers and beings. (A mere handful of titles culled from the last few years includes *Charmed, Being Human, True Blood, American Horror Story, Fringe, Medium, Grimm, Merlin, Heroes, Game of Thrones, Supernatural*, and the list goes on.) Yet, the ways in which such magical universes capture popular attention are not unlike the ways in which earlier generations of Americans were captivated by the mystery and alleged primitiveness of non-Western religious traditions—in particular those connected with Native America and Western Africa. With regard to the latter, the frightening specter of "black magic" and "witchcraft" was expressed in a fascination among European and Euro-American whites with Vodou (Haiti), and its sister African Caribbean traditions: Obeah (Jamaica), Santeria (Cuba, Central America), and Candomblé (Brazil). All of these religions are related through a common descent from slaves taken from Yoruba, Igbo, Ewe, and Fon peoples. While examination of these traditions has shown them to be complex, subtle, and symbolically rich, it continues to be the case that they are regarded by many as both superstitious and primitive; their "magic" derived from a lack of reasoning and knowledge. The distinctions between magic, witchcraft, and sorcery are, in this understanding, blurry to say the least. We should not let the obvious differences between such pop cultural phenomena as the *Harry Potter* novels and films and Haitian Vodou obscure what these have in common—that they are attractive in part because they exude a quality of mystery and unknown power that defies conventional rationality. In the case of Rowling's novels, this is unproblematic. But when discussing the authentic religious worlds of living, vibrant societies that have been historically marginalized and culturally dominated (to say the very least), it is hopefully clear how treating such beliefs and rituals as mysterious in contemporary times might hinder rather than help advance an appreciation of these as fully formed and culturally sophisticated religions. It is hard to see how the idea of magic, applied to such historically rich traditions, can be helpful in advancing our knowledge of them.

Returning to the theme of magic in U.S. popular culture, the portrayal of magical culture in media and entertainment—books, film, television series, onstage spectacles and performance—is of course nothing new; it has been happening for many decades. What *is* new is the extent to which the supernatural and natural worlds are increasingly being explained in terms of one another. While the *Harry Potter* universe has tended to leave to the readers' and viewers' imaginations the question of how magic happens, other popular depictions—among them the *Star Wars* and *Star Trek* sagas—increasingly endeavor to account for what might otherwise be inexplicable powers and events in terms of scientific reality. Consider the way in which the mystical concept of "The Force" in George Lucas's *Star Wars* films underwent a metamorphosis between the original film trilogy (late 1970s and early 1980s) and the second (late 1990s and early 2000s). Rather than leave this transcendent power unexplained, the later films sought to ground it in ideas drawn from genetics, microbiology, and other advanced scientific fields. Lucas put a new spin on the older, vaguely religious idea of an all-powerful and perhaps inscrutable universal essence by invoking fictional microorganisms—"midi-chlorians"—that mediated between the Force and human physiology, bestowing great power on certain individuals. For our discussion, what matters is that Lucas was almost certainly tapping into a blossoming millennial fascination with highly advanced technologies that would seem to hold the promise of uniting theology and science. The appeal of a unified theory of everything is increasingly attractive to a generation disenchanted by the many controversies, scandals, and perceived hypocrisies of traditional religious institutions. Popular sagas like the *Star Wars* films help to articulate this discontent by providing a more satisfactory, if less spiritually demanding, alternative to formal religion that simultaneously generates great excitement and cinematic drama. The lure of the magical—transcendent power available and at work in this world—is almost certainly a key driver of this appeal.

On this note, I cannot complete this introduction without mention of Walt Disney's "magic kingdom." In the nineteenth century, French sociologist Émile Durkheim famously discussed the power of social ritual to generate a transcendent emotional and physiological experience of what he called "collective effervescence." Perhaps no better single instance of this experience in U.S. culture can be found than the vast, multi-platform and impressively lucrative world of Disney films, theme parks, television, music, and toys. If we expand Durkheim's idea to incorporate the ritualization of everyday childhood activities, centered on viewing movies and television, listening to and singing songs, playing video games, playing with toys, and dressing up in glittering, character-themed costumes, it is clear that the effervescent emotion he referred to is real for children—many millions of whom experience this imagined world across multiple domains. But even if we consider solely the in-person social community that forms at Disney theme parks (closer to what Durkheim had in mind), it is clear what the term magic is intended to convey when applied to this context.

Recent visits to Disneyland with my daughter and several of her young schoolmates leave little doubt in my mind as to the impact of this place on a child's imagination. Developmentally, children are emotionally and physiologically receptive to new vistas of spectacle, sound, and color; the thrill that comes from encountering beloved storybook characters; eating normally verboten foods in abundance (cotton candy, soda, and massive ice cream cones for dinner, anyone?); and experiencing out-of-the-ordinary events in an out-of-the-ordinary way. (Riding thrilling roller coasters at nighttime and watching colorful parades well into the evening come to mind.) What is this powerful, transformative experience if *not* magic? The term is appropriate in relation both to the storybook fairytales of the Disney universe and to the impact of these in the context of overwhelming theme park experiences. Acquisition by Disney Studios of parallel "magical" universes in the form of Pixar films and characters, Marvel Comics heroes and all the vast world of Star Wars seems poised to generate new synergies of transcendent experience, particularly for children (and, as the expression goes, "children at heart").

While many have wondered whether religion is being eroded by a non-religious or secular society, one might just as easily ask whether or not it is really the character of public interest in the transcendent that has changed (together with its rituals, heroes, and institutions), rather than its fundamental appeal. While it cannot be denied that there is an ongoing tension in U.S. society between commitment to traditional forms of religion and newer, media-driven, "non-religious" religions like Star Wars, Harry Potter, Star Trek, and Disney, neither can the emotional and socially compelling character of these forms of secular (yet transcendently oriented) "magic" be ignored.

BELIEVERS FLOCK TO VIRGIN MARY STATUE "CRYING" RED TEARS

RICH PEDRONCELLI

Carrying rosary beads and cameras, the faithful have been coming in a steady stream to a church on the outskirts of Sacramento for a glimpse of what some are calling a miracle: A statue of the Virgin Mary they say has begun crying a substance that looks like blood.

It was first noticed more than a week ago, when a priest at the Vietnamese Catholic Martyrs Church spotted a stain on the statue's face and wiped it away. Before Mass on Nov. 20, people again noticed a reddish substance near the eyes of the white concrete statue outside the small church, said Ky Truong, 56, a parishioner.

Since then, Truong said he has been at the church day and night, so emotional he can't even work. He believes the tears are a sign.

"There's a big event in the future—earthquake, flood, a disease," Truong said. "We're very sad."

On Saturday, tables in front of the fenced-in statue were jammed with potted plants, bouquets of roses and candles. Some people prayed silently, while others sang hymns and hugged their children. An elderly woman in a wheelchair wept near the front of the crowd.

A red trail could be seen from the side of the statue's left eye to about halfway down the robe of concrete.

"I think that it's incredible. It's a miracle. Why is she doing it? Is it something bothering her?" asked Maria Vasquez, 35, who drove with her parents and three children from Stockton, about 50 miles south of Sacramento.

Thousands of such incidents are reported around the world each year, though many turn out to be hoaxes or natural phenomena.

The Diocese of Sacramento has so far not commented on the statue, and the two priests affiliated with the church did not return a telephone message Saturday.

The Rev. James Murphy, deacon of the diocese's mother church, the Cathedral of the Blessed Sacrament, said church leaders are always skeptical at first.

"For people individually seeing things through the eyes of faith, something like this can be meaningful. As for whether it is supernatural or a miracle, normally these incidences are not. Miracles are possible, of course," Murphy said. "The bishop is just waiting and seeing what happens. They will be moving very slowly."

But seeing the statue in person left no doubt for Martin Operario, 60, who drove about 100 miles from Hayward. He took photos to show to family and friends.

"I don't know how to express what I'm feeling," Operario said. "Since religion is the mother of believing, then I believe."

Nuns Anna Bui and Rosa Hoang, members of the Salesian Sisters of San Francisco, also made the trek Saturday. Whether the weeping statue is declared a miracle or not, they said, it is already doing good by awakening people to the faith and reminding them to pray.

"It's a call for us to change ourselves, to love one another," Hoang said.

|||||||||||||||||||||||||||||||||||||||||||||||||||||||||||||||||||||

HOW WALT DISNEY MADE AMERICA INTO A MAGIC KINGDOM

GIL TROY

Sixty years after it opened, Disneyland—and its subsequent iterations— shows how one man rebranded America into Happy Land

Slow-starters, take heart! If Walt Disney had defined Disneyland by its opening day performance 60 years ago on July 17, 1955, he would have been Dis-heartened and Dis-missed his $17 million theme park as a Dis-aster.

In what he later called "Black Sunday," 28,000 visitors mobbed the park; as many as 17,000 had counterfeit tickets. Traffic backed up for 7 miles approaching the 160-acre plot of land near Anaheim that just 365 days earlier had been orange groves. Kids relieved themselves in the parking lot. Ladies struggled to extricate their high heels from the asphalt that melted in the 100-degree heat. With a plumbers' strike having forced Disney to choose between finishing the bathrooms or the water fountains, "Uncle Walt" had calculated, only partially correctly, that "People can buy Pepsi-Cola, but they can't pee in the street."

Undeterred, the indomitable Disney proclaimed: "To all who come to this happy place, welcome. Disneyland is your land." And with his magical touch, the "cast members" welcomed the million plus "guests" who arrived in the first seven weeks warmly and craftily. Clumps of weeds had signs designating them by their fancy-sounding Latin names. The two-story mound of dirt generated by digging out the moat around the soon-to-be-iconic Fantasyland castle became "Lookout Mountain."

This commitment to making Disneyland—and all its subsequent satellites—"the happiest place on earth"—reflected a broader post-Great Depression, post-World War II attempt to make America into Happy Camp. Before, American culture was traditionally Puritanical, thrifty, hardworking, and sober, more Horatio Alger than Mickey Mouse. With the country prospering and with entertainment technologies becoming ever more omnipresent, Disney and especially Disneyland helped make our popular culture more indulgent, spendthrift, distracted, and—dare we say it—goofy.

The Mouseketeers—who also debuted that day—captured the open yet exclusive democratic-capitalist genius of Disney and his land by singing: "Who's the leader of the club that's made for you and me…" (Television's *Mickey Mouse Club* began that October). With more free time and more disposable income in a growing leisure culture, Americans loved Disneyland's old-fashioned, accessible populism, and the validation they felt when they actually arrived, then survived interminable lines to experience super-popular rides. Spending an average $5 a day—today admission alone can be $100 a person, err, guest—Americans could feel like kings and queens while celebrating the Main Street values they feared America was losing, even in Eisenhower's 1950s.

Then, as now, Disney peddled the fantasy of America's eternal innocence. New York was the cultural capital of an America enjoying its post-World War II high, defined by men in their gray flannel suits and happy homemakers in their white gloves, even at amusement parks. Yet the Baby Boomers' cultural revolution was stirring. Jack Kerouac, the Beats, and Mad magazine's zany satirists were already writing. Bill Haley and the Comets' breakthrough Rock Around the Clock had just hit No. 1 on the *Billboard* charts July 9 and would remain there for eight weeks, throughout the summer of '55. By 1956, Elvis would be rocking 'n' rolling.

As America's gravitas started fading, its center of gravity was shifting south and west: Disney's California home was becoming America's Fantasyland. In 1957 the New York Giants and the Brooklyn Dodgers would even abandon the Big Apple for the Golden State.

In a delicious touch, Ronald Reagan was one of the movie stars working with Walt Disney and 22 ABC-TV cameras to introduce Disneyland to a record-breaking 90 million viewers that day. Although not yet a politician, Reagan shared Disney's sensibility. Both were Midwest provincials who celebrated the region each had escaped. Both mentally inhabited a world where the jungle was about animals chased by natives chanting "ooga-booga"—Adventureland! Space travel was about the "gee whiz" thrill of it all—Tomorrowland! Main Street was sanitized and commoditized, and all Americans dreamed of living in a gadget-filled home version of the Carousel of Progress, just like the one General Electric built for the Reagans in the 1950s. The Carousel became a Disneyland hit in 1967.

In Disney's world, American history was a triumphal march of progress to uphold the Framers' ideals. As Frontierland opened, with the "cast" dancing around in a Disneyfied square dance style, Fess Parker as Davy Crockett rhapsodized about "my one and only Besty," his rifle. Now-politically offensive lines included: "40 arrows hit a tree and I knew the Sioux were out for me. Now-politically naïve lines included: "I use it for defendin' me, I shoot for life and liberty."

This enduring faith in America explains how Disneyland and its empire expanded. Rather than going the way of black-and-white TVs, phonographs, *Ozzie and Harriet*, rotary telephones, hi-fis, Studebakers, the $1 minimum wage, and the Cold War, Disney mass-marketed his optimistic faith that "when you wish upon a star your dreams come true."

Cultural historian Warren Susman believed that Mickey Mouse's escapism better explained why there was no revolution during the Great Depression than Franklin Roosevelt's reforms, and so Disneyland became one of postwar America's defining institutions. It was immersive—anticipating today's 24/7 virtual entertainment barrage wherein popular culture is everywhere and forever. It was a synergistic, mass shopping experience, monetizing our childhoods and our dreams with movies boosting theme parks boosting characters boosting merchandise and on and on in a perpetual consumerist spin cycle. And in eternally recycling the past, blending yesterday, today, and tomorrow into one happy romp, Disneyland mass-produced memories and commodified our identities—for a hefty, but just affordable, price tag. All this was a natural consequence of Walt Disney's first magic trick in the 1920s and 1930s: taming Europe's grim Grimm Fairy Tales, giving them upbeat, life-affirming, all-American happy endings, in Technicolor.

Sixty revolutionary years later, despite all our postmodern cynicism and Internet-era sophistication, Disneyland's first five regions still reflect five enduring pillars of the American dream. We want our lives to be as magical and exciting as Mickey's and Minnie's in Fantasyland and as the boldest hunters in Adventureland. We still venerate Davy Crockett's pioneering values in Frontierland. And we still want to come home again, reassured by the tranquility of Main Street USA, even as we forge bigger and better Tomorrowlands.

Ultimately, despite many faults, America remains a Magic Kingdom, a remarkable experiment in creating the world's first mass middle-class civilization, seeking to make as many people as possible as rich and free as possible. Disneyland—and now the entire Disney world—for all its marketing manipulations and capitalist exploitations—reminds us that, compared to where we once were as a country, and where most people still are worldwide, when you wish upon the stars—and stripes—many of your dreams really can and do come true.

III

WHY BABIES (AND PERHAPS ALL OF US) CARE ABOUT MAGIC

SUSANA MARTINEZ-CONDE

[handwritten: Just as magic acts aren't real, "magic" is not real and is there to take away from reality.]

We base our everyday behavior on thousands of predictions about how reality will unfold around us as we interact with our physical and social environment. Some of our expectations are the product of hard-won experience and direct interaction with the world. Other expectations are programmed in infancy, and hard-wired into our neural systems with little or no exposure to external stimulation. Scientists refer to the latter set of expectations as "core knowledge". Some examples of it are our understanding that solids will not go through walls, or that objects will fall if dropped.

Magic acts hinge on defying all sorts of expectations about the way things should be. Confronted with the violation of their core predictions, audiences become captivated. The most jaded spectator can feel a kind of childlike wonder in front of a talented magician. A new research study investigating how babies react to violations of their prior expectations may explain why magic is so compelling to audiences of all ages.

Aimee E. Stahl and Lisa Feigenson from Johns Hopkins University thought that violations of one's expectations about the world might signal special opportunities for learning. Previous research had shown that babies stare for longer times when their expectations are violated; for instance, if a ball appears to pass through a wall rather than being stopped by the wall, or when an actor approaches someone mean rather than someone nice. It was not known however, whether the babies' increased interest in entities that didn't behave as they should had any cognitive utility.

The scientists hypothesized that violations of expectations might provide opportunities to learn about the world. If so, infants should preferentially learn new information about objects that violate expectations, seek information about those objects, and explore the objects in such a way as to test possible explanations for their bizarre behavior.

The researchers tested one hundred and ten 11-month-old infants in an elegant series of experiments. First, the babies watched as toy cars or balls went through walls or were stopped by them (among other physically possible and impossible scenarios). Then, the scientists showed the babies something new about the object they had just observed: for instance, that it squeaked when pushed. The babies learned to associate the sound with the object only if the object had violated their expectations previously. This meant that learning was not generally enhanced following a violation-scenario, but was restricted to the specific objects that violated the babies' expectations.

Next, the scientists had the babies watch events that were either congruent with, or in violation of, basic principles such as object solidity (the object appeared to pass through walls) and object support (the object appeared to hover unsupported in midair). Then, the infants had the opportunity to explore and play with the object they had just watched (the target object) and also with a new object (distractor object). The babies spent more time exploring the target object if it had previously violated core principles. When the object behaved consistently with their expectations, babies played equally with the target and distractor objects. Even more fascinating, the children interacted with target objects that had violated expectations in ways that critically depended on the type of violation observed. The babies who had seen the object go through a wall banged it repeatedly against the table, as if testing its consistency, whereas the babies that had seen the object float in the air dropped it over and over again. That is, the kids tailored their explorations to the type of violation witnessed. This dissociation indicates that the babies were not just reacting in random ways to the surprising scenarios, but were systematically testing their environments, much as scientists do when puzzled by an unpredicted piece of data.

The study concluded that violations of expectations, whether learned or innate, provide special learning opportunities in babyhood and early childhood.

But what about adults confronting the unexpected?

As adults, we don't often experience radical violations of our expectations, particularly those that concern core principles of object behavior. One important exception is magic—a magic performance turns our reasonable expectations upside down: objects vanish, levitate and metamorphose. What if each of these violations signals a unique learning opportunity not only to the infant brain but to the adult brain as well? It may be that magic performances are so compelling because we are wired to engage our minds and actions in unexpected situations.

At the Magic of Consciousness Symposium that Stephen Macknik and I co-hosted in 2007 in Las Vegas, Teller, the mute half of the magician duo Penn and Teller, eloquently proposed that much of our lives is devoted to understanding cause and effect, and that magic "provides a playground for those rational skills". A baby's playground is as large as the world, filled with everyday wonder and opportunity. As we age and learn, the amazement and playfulness shrinks—but we can always rely on magic for a visitor's pass to the stunning playground of the mind.

ARTICLE 16

IS RELIGION GOOD FOR CHILDREN?

Secular Children Differ in Happiness, Mental Health, and Their Grasp of Reality

MARK JOSEPH STERN

I n the United States, conventional wisdom holds that you should raise your child to be religious. Taking the kids to church is the default; leaving them home requires justification. Push parents to explain why they should pass on their religion—apart from a principled urge to keep the faith—and they're likely to tell you studies prove that kids do better with religion than without it.

But is religion really good for kids? That might depend on what kind of child you want to raise.

Several studies do seem to corroborate the conventional wisdom that kids raised with religion—any religion—are psychologically healthier than kids raised without it. The gap here is small but real: Some researchers link religious affiliation and regular church attendance with a mild boost in children's mental health. That data is reported by parents, though, which presents an obvious problem: Religious parents might simply be more inclined than secular parents to view their kids through rose-colored stained glass. But teachers have also reported that kids who attend religious services have stronger self-control and react better to discipline.

One reason why children in religious families might be better behaved is that they think there's more at stake. According to the so-called sanctification theory, religion imbues familial relationships with sacred significance, and religious institutions attach moral meaning to certain behaviors. Religious parents might see childrearing as sacred work and strive to raise kids with self-control and manners. Religious kids might also see good behavior as a moral imperative and strive to maintain discipline, not just for their own sake, but to please their parents—and God.

But the question of causality claws at researchers' confidence in these findings and theories. John Bartkowksi, a professor of sociology at University of Texas at San Antonio, wonders whether church attendance really leads to good behavior—or whether it might be the other way around.

"It may be that kids who are already well-behaved are the only ones who can get into religious communities," Bartkowski told me. "Their parents might feel they'll fit in because they're compliant and able to sit still." Self-control, in other words, might lead to church service, and not vice versa.

One other related possibility of many is that religious parents may have more respect for authority, and they may reinforce obedience in their children more than secular parents do.

Based on this research, you might think that raising religious children is neutral at worst, preferable at best, and probably worth the hassle of dragging the kids out of bed every Sunday. But there are some major pitfalls on the parental road to Damascus. Parents who argue over religion can actually make their children less happy and more disobedient—so make sure you and your spouse have settled the great transubstantiation vs. consubstantiation debate before taking your kid to Mass. Fundamentalist and conservative religions, moreover, run the risk of teaching kids who violate dogma to hate themselves. If you tell your gay child he's "intrinsically disordered" because of his identity, or exorcise him of the "demon of homosexuality," his mental health is likely to be quite low.

Aside from these obvious drawbacks, there's another, subtler problem with raising religious children: All that talk of snake-inspired subterfuge, planet-cleansing floods, and apocalyptic horsemen might hamper kids' ability to differentiate between fantasy and reality—or even to think critically.

That's the implication of two recent studies published in *Cognitive Science* in which researchers attempted to gauge perceptions of reality in religious and secular children. (The religious children were all from Christian families, from a variety of denominations.) In one study, the researchers read realistic stories and fantasy tales to the kids. Some of the fantasy tales featured familiar biblical events—like the parting of the Red Sea—but with non-biblical characters. (In the retelling of the Red Sea story, Moses was called John.) Others featured non-biblical but clearly magical events—the parting of a mountain, for instance—as well as non-biblical characters.

In another study, the researchers read children three different versions of the same story. One version had a biblical character performing a miracle, like Jonah escaping a whale's stomach, and noted that God was behind the miracle. A second version told of the same miraculous event, but left out any mention of God. A third retold the story realistically, with no miracles and no God.

Every child believed that the protagonist of the realistic stories was a real person. But when asked about the stories featuring biblically inspired or non-biblical but magical events, the children disagreed. Children raised with religion thought the protagonists of the miraculous stories were real people, and they seemed to interpret the narratives—both biblical and magical—as true accounts.

Secular children, on the other hand, were quick to perceive that these stories were fictitious, construing them as fairy tales rather than real-life narratives. They had a far keener sense of reality than religious children, who failed to understand that magic does not exist and believed that stories describing magical details such as "invisible sails" could be real. Secular kids generally understood that any story featuring magic could not take place in the world they inhabit.

To the researchers behind the study, this division in perceptions of reality was striking. "Religious teaching," they wrote, "especially exposure to miracle stories, leads children to a more generic receptivity toward the impossible, that is, a more wide-ranging acceptance that the impossible can happen in defiance of ordinary causal relations." "when you wish upon a star!"

If you're surprised by these findings, you probably haven't attended a church service lately. Religions tend to be *founded* on miracle stories—exactly the thing religious kids had trouble distinguishing from reality. When you've been told that a woman was created from a man's rib, or that a man reawakened three days postmortem little worse for wear, your grasp on reality is bound to take a hit. Religious children are told these stories from an early age, often as though they are unquestionably true. (Some are told that questioning them might lead to eternal damnation.) If you're expected to believe two of every animal could fit on an ark made of gopher wood, wouldn't you have trouble understanding that magical sails don't exist?

It's still unclear, of course, exactly how seriously religion hinders kids' perceptions of reality; the children in the latest study were 3 to 6 years old, so the effect could fade as kids garner more complex critical thinking skills. And some researchers aren't so sure the study's results can be extrapolated. Paul Bloom, a professor of psychology at Yale, called it "a cool study by a sharp research team," but note that most kids, religious or secular, are pretty good at distinguishing fantasy from reality.

"For the most part, children only look incompetent when dealing with the stories of clever psychologists," Bloom told me. He also noted that children are frequently exposed to seemingly incredible things that also happen to be true, such as evolution and plate tectonics, which can force them to re-evaluate their perceptions of reality.

"The problem with certain religious beliefs," according to Bloom, "isn't that they are incredible (science is also incredible) and isn't that they ruin children's ability to distinguish between fantasy and reality. It's that they are false."

That's the problem that undergirds pretty much every study about religion and happiness: Even if religion *can* make you happy, that happiness often requires us to buy into fantasies. It's no coincidence that the most statistically significant mental health difference between religious and secular children arises between the age of 12 and 15, when nondevout kids go through the existential crises of adolescence while religious kids can dig deeper into their trench of piousness. This mental health bump disappears in adulthood, when religious people—perhaps because they're operating in the real world—aren't measurably happier or nicer than their secular brethren (unless they live in a country that favors believers and ostracizes atheists).

The question of children and religion, then, is really just a small part of the broader dilemma of faith versus skepticism. In the United States, the vast majority of us choose the former and push our kids to do the same. That might make them docile, obliging, and credulous. But it doesn't make them better people.

Discussion Questions

1. Describe the phenomenon of the "weeping statue." Why do you think this phenomenon is appealing, and how do church officials feel about it? Would you consider this phenomenon to be "magical"?

2. Walt Disney, together with the culture and institutions he founded, has sold a vision of a magical universe to generations of Americans—especially children. Do you believe this is a socially healthy (or beneficial) aspect of consumer culture? What *is* Disney magic, exactly, and what does the Disney universe of ideas and characters say about broader American notions of what a perfect society would look like?

3. What is "core knowledge," and what does its presence or absence mean for beliefs about magic? What about infancy, in particular, is important for understanding the experience of magic?

4. In what ways does traditional religious education and observance promote magical thinking in children? Is this detrimental to their socialization as rational adults, and their ability to distinguish fantasy from reality? Even if this is the case, does it matter? Why? Why not?

Further Readings

1. Douglas Brode. *Multiculturalism and the Mouse: Race and Sex in Disney Entertainment*. Austin: University of Texas Press, 2005.
   In this work, Brode asserts that Disney's legacy is one of burgeoning cultural diversity (and not the utopic imaginings of white, middle-class America, as many have argued). He also maintains that sexual equality, feminism, and women's empowerment were central to the

Disney aesthetic decades before they achieved political legitimacy within U.S. culture.

2. Alan Bryman. *The Disneyization of Society*. Thousand Oaks, CA: SAGE Publications, 2004.

Bryman's book investigates the ways in which Disney's imagined universe and theme parks establish a template for "themed" environments (such as those focused on gambling, shopping, zoos, and hotels), in which social activity, labor, and consumption of goods and services are streamlined and harmonized within a carefully managed and surveilled environment.

3. Brian P. Copenhaver. *Magic in Western Culture: From Antiquity to Enlightenment*. Cambridge University Press, 2015.

A comprehensive survey of magic practice and belief from the ancient Mediterranean and Near East through medieval and early modern Europe. Copenhaver treats magic as a coherent intellectual and philosophical tradition, rather than a marginal aspects of religious studies.

4. Kevin S. Decker, Jason T. Eberl, and William Irwin, eds. *Star Wars and Philosophy: More Powerful than You Can Possibly Imagine*. Chicago: Open Court, 2005.

A series of essays by philosophers on a range of topics that are linked to the *Star Wars* universe of characters and themes. These include such perennial themes as the problem of evil, freedom versus predestination, environmental ethics, and the meanings of democracy and tyranny.

5. Émile Durkheim. *Elementary Forms of the Religious Life*. Oxford Classics, 2008.

Durkheim's *Elementary Forms* is among a handful of foundational texts in the sociological and anthropological study of religion. In it, he marshals ethnographic examples from a host of contexts to build his case that religion is cultivated through a profound experience of collective social performance and the effervescent sense of the "sacred" that collective ritual generates.

6. Annette Hill. *Paranormal Media: Audiences, Spirits and Magic in Popular Culture.* Abingdon, UK: Routledge, 2010.

An introduction to the recent mainstreaming of ideas about the transcendent and paranormal in contemporary Anglo-US culture, Hill explores changes in how people have sought to have direct experience of spirits and magical power from the nineteenth through twenty-first centuries. Such encounters range from relatively direct participation through ghost hunting and use of psychic mediums, to sustained interest in transcendent-themed television shows and theatrical films.

7. Joe Nickell. *Looking for a Miracle: Weeping Icons, Relics, Stigmata, Visions, and Healing Cures.* Amherst, NY: Prometheus Books, 1999.

In this accessible work written for a non-specialist readership, popular historian Nickell examines the scientific and cultural bases for a large range of examples drawn from the world of magical faith healing. Specifically, he seeks to examine the hard evidence behind claims concerning visions, weeping statues, and other miracles. In so doing, he hopes to understand whether credulous people have been duped, or whether they have insight that transcends the pronouncements of science.

LIVING WITH
THE EVIL DEAD

SECTION FOUR
INTRODUCTION

Among the most popular supernatural beings to adorn the imaginations of modern Westerners are those creatures we variously assign to the categories ghost, zombie, vampire, and demon. Arguably, in the modern United States, such creatures receive far more attention and popular acclaim than gods and other "higher powers." While this would of course seem blasphemous to some, it is clear from the abundance of novels, television series, feature films, video games, and other media that there is an abiding fascination in "other-than-human" persons, to employ anthropologist Irving Hallowell's phrase. In the Western religious traditions (and beyond), angels and saints often stir up similar fascination and devotion. Still, it is mostly to the darker and morally ambiguous creatures, and not to the fixtures of religious tradition, that popular U.S. culture turns when seeking excitement and the thrill of otherworldliness.

The creature we call the zombie has enjoyed a long history within horror films, comic books, and other pulp fiction. At the time of this writing, zombies are enjoying something of a renaissance on the small screen in AMC's critically acclaimed series *The Walking Dead*. Other recent, big-budget incarnations have included 2004's *Dawn of the Dead* and the popular *28 Days/Weeks After* and *Resident Evil* series. In the imagination of popular culture, zombies terrify for their "inhuman" natures. Once human, they are now either dead flesh or diseased beyond repair. Perhaps the most terrifying of their traits is their insatiable hunger for living human flesh. In these ways, the cinematic zombie embodies some of the deepest terrors possible for human beings: a complete loss of life and humanity symbolized by cannibalism (after all, the terror, though real, would doubtless be less jarring if these creatures were feral cats and not human beings). While full discussion of the origins of the zombie concept are beyond the scope of this introduction, the Haitian zombie—a shambling, soulless figure to be pitied more than feared—provides a clue as to just how far Western culture has departed from original ideas concerning the living dead. In the Haitian countryside, where zombification has served historically as a form of capital punishment for antisocial behavior, the deepest fear imaginable is not *of* zombies, but of *becoming* a zombie. In Western culture, this nuance has been upended: being dead-yet-alive has its own terrors that have little to do with depriving individuals of an afterlife. The popular American zombie embodies not just the deepest fears of the animalistic in humanity, but also reflects ideas about an apocalyptic end to human society—invariably, zombie stories invoke ideas about great punishment against all humans for our sins. In this sense, they reflect a sobering moral caution of the Judeo-Christian tradition.

Vampires play something of a different role in the popular imagination, and consequently their stature in the media of film, television, and books is different from that of the zombie. In 1897, Bram Stoker's seminal fictional creation, Count Dracula, certainly embodied late Victorian ideas about the dangerous, primitive, and wild reaches of southeastern Europe, and was a true portrait of terror (Stoker's description of the creature emphasizes animalistic and inhuman features … the long teeth, cruel expression, hairy palms, and so on). But beginning with Bela Lugosi's classic big-screen portrayal of Dracula in 1931, the vampiric image was inflected with sophistication and elegance. These manifestly positive characteristics were augmented in later decades by still more surreal departures from the horrific. Over the last several decades, fictional vampires have rarely been depicted as monsters. Instead, they are romantic anti-heroes and social outsiders: author Anne Rice's vampires, those of the teen-oriented *Twilight* stories and films, and the sultry southerners of HBO's *True Blood* stand out in this reformulation. In the *Blade* films and short-lived television series, and in *Buffy the Vampire Slayer*, protagonists are even promoted to the ranks of superhero.

This metamorphosis of the vampire in popular culture away from horror and toward gothic, romantic heroism is an interesting turn. Unlike zombies, vampires generally embody admired human qualities;

among them, intelligence, physical beauty, and cultural sophistication. More often than not, they are highly sexualized beings whose capacity to seduce mere mortals is part of their appeal. This is worlds away from the authentic zombie-like vampires of eastern-European folklore, which, more often than not, depicts these creatures as feared scavengers, widow makers, and cradle robbers. Modern media has been responsible for this transformation, but it has flourished because such revised creatures reflect not just human fears, but human desires. The longing for immortal life, beauty, and strength is achieved in vampire fiction, even though it is at a cost—an endless thirst for human blood. Could the enduring appeal of vampires be related to our ambivalence about our own moral standing, as evidenced by the fact that these creatures are at once supernaturally evil and the "ideal" of what a human life might be?

In contrast to zombies and vampires, ghosts and demons—like angels and saints—enjoy "official" status within a variety of religious institutions, in that they are viewed as real—and sometimes dangerous. In popular entertainment, depictions of these range from the fantastical (the beings that maraud Hogwarts castle in J.K. Rowling's widely acclaimed film and book series *Harry Potter*, for instance) to "realistic" portrayals of spirit possession of human beings. It is on this point that we see a sharp departure from zombie and vampire lore in the popular imagination. While most (not all) concede, however reluctantly, that zombies and vampires don't actually exist, ghosts and demons are often treated as potentially real. This is reinforced in too many horror films to count, but also in the past two decades by such "reality" programming as the SyFy Channel's *Ghost Hunters* and documentary-style films as *The Blair Witch Project* (1999) and *Paranormal Activity* (2007). It is not just reality-style productions that reinforce belief in ghosts, but also feature films that are fictional but sufficiently tinged with or inspired by "real" events as to provoke profound dread, where vampire and zombie films might not. And, in one article included in Section IV, while CNN is a "respected news source" watched by millions, the network tantalizes viewers by appearing agnostic (that is, neither believing nor unbelieving) on the question of haunted houses. In this way, their objective reportage moves ever closer to that of "reality" shows that seek out the paranormal not to educate, but to entertain.

In U.S. society a 1973 film, *The Exorcist*, has been prominent in reifying ideas about the demonic in popular culture. In it, we are introduced not solely to the demonic but also to the orientation of Roman Catholicism toward the demonic. The following example illustrates how the ambivalence of a "modern" Church to "medieval" ritual becomes a theological problem that must be solved in order to save a little girl's life. In one scene, a character named Chris MacNeil is speaking with a Catholic priest, Father Damien Karrass, about her daughter, Regan. MacNeil is at her wit's end and, though not religious, has approached a priest for help when modern medical science and psychology seem to have failed. The problem, she explains, is that Regan has apparently been possessed by an evil spirit. At first hesitant, MacNeil confesses her hope that Karrass might arrange an exorcism to drive the demon away and so cure her daughter. Dumbfounded, Karrass explains that she probably knows as much as he about exorcism, and that in order to do things properly, they would have to invent a time machine and travel back to the sixteenth century! Her turn to be surprised; MacNeil is incredulous. Since when do Catholic priests not know how to perform exorcisms? Ever since, Karrass explains patiently, the world learned about mental illness and anxiety disorders.

This tension within the modern Catholic Church between scientific rationalism and an undercurrent of conviction in the real existence of the Devil and his minions provides a dramatic backdrop against which the plot of *The Exorcist* advances. In the broader context of Western culture, this question has a quality of seriousness to it that is absent from considerations of zombies and vampires. Demons and demonic forces are considered to be objectively real, and this is reflected in the sober tenor of how such creatures are portrayed—even in fiction.

The articles in section four approach the phenomena described above from several vantages. Vampire role-playing games gain popularity on a university campus, while "real" vampires claim to inhabit the darker spaces of New Orleans, "objective" news reporting embraces (or at least flirts with) the idea of hauntings, and fictional zombies provoke widespread speculation of global catastrophe. In this media-driven cacophony of perspectives and questions, convictions and fears, students of such phenomena might well ask whether or not supernatural beings like ghosts, zombies, vampires, and demons have now transcended their own fictionalization to become culturally real in a way that will shape religious and otherworldly knowledge and awareness in decades to come.

|||||||||||||||||||||||||||||||||||||||||||||||||||||||||||||||||

CNN REPORTERS ATTACKED BY GHOSTS LIVE ON AIR!

MOVIEPILOT

The words "COME HERE…" were caught on tape as a ghostly voice whispers to a CNN cameraman. A history of grisly deaths, ghosts and demons. Is this one of the most haunted houses in the U.S.?

A routine video interview took a sinister turn for this group of CNN reporters last summer, as each crew member is attacked and physically harassed by an unseen presence. This house in Pennsylvania is reported to have a whole host of ghosts and ghouls haunting it.

These apparitions have apparently haunted the family for years, they have even been known to attack the family pets. Ghostly voices, shrieks, and screams often cut through the night's silence. The report suggests that the spirits are very antagonistic and do not respond well to any human presence within what is probably regarded as 'their house.'

Things get much darker as you delve deeper into the house. The basement of this home holds within it an even more insidious being. A demon is rumoured to haunt this area, recorded in a photo and dubbed 'Shadow man' this demon looks to be a whopping seven feet tall.

What are we seeing here?

What is apparently showcased within this house is what's known as an "Intelligent Haunting" consisting of both human and nonhuman entities.

An intelligent haunting is a recorded haunting in which it would seem that the entity is aware of the physical world. This situation allows the entity to interact with us here in the present. It allows for physical interaction with anything from inanimate objects, doors to even people.

The difference between a human and nonhuman haunting is pretty much as it sounds, a human haunting seems to be the spirit or presence of an entity that was, at one point, human.

A non human entity is something considerably different. A nonhuman specter can be considered to be an angel or demon for example. These beings have infinitely more power and influence on the physical world than any other entity. These forms of beings have been documented in countries and continents around the world since time began.

We all love a good scare every now and again, this latest piece is not directly linked to gaming I know but with the second DLC releasing next month from the world renowned survival horror game The Evil Within I thought that a little horror hype wouldn't hurt.

Known as "The Consequence", it will wrap up the story that began with "The Assignment." Bethesda has not shed any light on "The Consequence" right now but it will release on both consoles and PC come April 21.

||||||||||||||||||||||||||||||||||||||||||||||||||||||||||||||||

THERE ARE TRIBES OF "VAMPIRE" PEOPLE IN NEW ORLEANS

JOHN EDGAR BROWNING

V ampires walk among us. But these people aren't the stuff of nightmares—far from it actually. Just sit down for a drink with one of them and ask for yourself. That's if you can find one. They aren't necessarily looking to be found.

I've spent five years conducting ethnographic studies of the real vampires living in New Orleans and Buffalo. They are not easy to find, but when you do track them down, they can be quite friendly.

"Real vampires" is the collective term by which these people are known. They're not "real" in the sense that they turn into bats and live forever but many do sport fangs and just as many live a primarily nocturnal existence. These are just some of the cultural markers real vampires adopt to express a shared (and, according to them, biological) essence—they need blood (human or animal) or psychic energy from donors in order to feel healthy.

Their self-described nature begins to manifest around or just after puberty. It derives, according to them, from the lack of subtle energies their bodies produce—energies other people take for granted. That's the general consensus anyway. It's a condition they claim to be unable to change. So, they embrace it.

The real vampire community, like the legendary figure it emulates, knows few national boundaries, from Russia and South Africa to England and the United States. Particularly in the internet age, vampires are often well attuned to community issues.

This is more true for some than others though. I found the vampires of Buffalo to be keen to keep up to date with the global community, while those in New Orleans were often more interested in the activities of their local vampire houses (an affiliated group of vampires usually led by a vampire elder who helps his or her house members to acclimate to their vampiric nature).

Some houses, and indeed whole vampire communities, as in the case of New Orleans, will combine their efforts to organise charity events, like feeding (not feeding on) the homeless. However, despite their humanitarian efforts, real vampires don't go around advertising who they are for fear of discrimination by people who simply don't understand them.

Some semblance of the real vampire community has existed since at least the early to mid-1970s, but my own dealings began in 2009 when I entered the New Orleans community clinging to my digital voice recorder.

I eventually met around 35 real vampires there, but the total number in New Orleans is easily double that. They ranged in age from 18 to 50 and represented both sexes equally. They practised sanguinarian (blood) and psychic feeding—taking energy using, for example, the mind or hands.

Blood is generally described by my study participants as tasting metallic, or "coppery" but can also be influenced by the donor's physiology, or even how well he or she is hydrated. Some psychic vampires use tantric feeding, that is through erotic or sexual encounters, while others use what could be described as astral feeding or feeding on another from afar. And others feed through emotion.

Afterwards, blood-drinking and psychic vampires feel energised or otherwise better than they would if they were to sustain themselves on regular food alone, like fruits, fish, and vegetables (which they eat too).

These vampires described themselves as atheistic, monotheistic or polytheistic. Some identified as heterosexual, some homosexual and some bisexual. Some were married, some were divorced, and some were parents.

Unquestionably, I found the vampires I met to be competent and generally outwardly "normal" citizens. They performed blood-letting rituals safely and only with willing donors and participated regularly in medical exams that scarcely (if ever) indicated complications from their feeding practises.

Tales of the unexpected

What was perhaps most surprising about the vampires I met though was their marked lack of knowledge about vampires in popular culture. They seemed to know much less than you might expect—at least for vampires—about how their kind were depicted in books and films. By this I mean to say that the people I met with and interviewed hadn't turned to drinking blood or taking psychic energy simply because they had read too many Anne Rice novels.

In fact, the real vampire community in general seems to have appropriated very few of the trappings mainstream culture attaches to creatures of the night. Many do dress in gothic clothes but certainly not all the time, and very, very few sleep in coffins. In fact, those vampire who do dress a certain way or wear fangs do so long after realising their desire to take blood.

This is what might be called a "defiant culture." Real vampires embrace their instinctual need to feed on blood or energy and use what mainstream culture sees as a negative, deviant figure like the vampire to achieve a sense of self-empowerment. They identify others with a similar need and have produced a community from that need.

But real vampires can also help us understand, and perhaps even shed, some of the ideological baggage each of us carries. They show us how repressive and oppressive categories can lead to marginalisation. Through them, we see the dark side of ourselves.

More generally, this community shows that being different doesn't have to force you onto the margins of society. Real vampires can and do exist in both "normal" society and their own communities, and that's okay.

SUCK FEST

ARTICLE 19

JONAH SPANGENTHAL-LEE

I t's a miserable, rainy Saturday night, but the vampires on the University of Washington's campus are out in force. The dimly lit outdoor atrium of a UW lecture hall looks like a cross between a casting call for the *Rocky Horror Picture Show* and the line for a Marilyn Manson concert as 50 pale, black-leather-clad Nosferatu skulk about. Human slaves are dragged across the concrete floor while their not-so-undead masters wander between groups discussing the imminent arrival of their new vampire prince. Every Saturday night, with fake European accents and fangs, these creatures swarm UW's Red Square to battle for imaginary territory and act out their deepest, darkest vampire fantasies. Players with monikers like "Razor" and "Nobody" are so dedicated to their personas that they spread out to chat about the politics of their imaginary world. Others throw down in player-versus-player combat, with games of rock, paper, scissors that can last up to an hour. Words for weapons, scrawled on dog-eared index cards, stand in for swords and guns to avoid confrontations with campus security.

Since 1995, UW's neo-gothic archways and dark corridors have been the feeding ground for members of the Emerald City Chronicles (ECC). Even among longtime players, there is debate over who started ECC, but its members have met consistently on Saturday nights, well after sunset, for more than a decade. They've had crushed garlic and water balloons thrown at them by obnoxious gawkers, but most of the time, they're left alone. Tonight's game is just another episode in the long-running role-playing saga. Players slowly advance their class and stature in vampire society, earning trinkets, weapons, human slaves, and, um, the tomes of the elders.

Standing in a dark stairwell, overlooking a group of a dozen ghost-hunting vampires, Janet Stiver, one of ECC's "assistant storytellers"—those who create and direct the flow of ECC's 12-year-old storyline, a battle between vampire clans for control of the "world of darkness"—addresses the perception that ECCers are all lifestyle-vampire weirdos. "It's hard to explain to someone who's like, 'Why do you do that?' Some people are [just] drawn to the romantic notion of vampires. We're fang dorks. It's like a huge stage with a bunch of characters," Stiver says. "It's a fight over food, standing, and control over the mortals. It's a release. We're just acting. You can come out here and be somebody else for a couple of hours."

As Stiver gushes about the benefits of pretending to be a vampire, a middle-aged man with leather gloves and a graying ponytail begins a "duel" with a leather-cuffed man in his mid 20s. "I'm gonna try an upper-cut," he says before they begin rock, paper, scissoring and spouting incomprehensible mathematical combat formulas. The winner claims the prestige of being an indomitable vampire warrior, and will hopefully walk away from the battle with a reward or two.

"Drake," a beefy 26-year-old with a long black ponytail and a long black trench coat, walks around the main game room—an angular, open-air, brick-lined hall—where 20 other vampires stand around talking, politicking, and speculating about the heir to the throne. Drake, who walks with a cane and speaks in a faux-British accent, has been part of ECC for the last five years "It's something to do on a Saturday night, other than getting drunk and waking up with a hangover," he says. Behind Drake, a young man wearing a black mask, a top hat, clunky leather boots, and Spock ears dances alone. There's no music playing. "There are a lot of weird people, but it's a community," Drake shrugs.

Indeed, ECC doubles as a tightly knit social club. According to Ross Skilling, another longtime player, "People have gotten jobs, relationships, and children out of this. I met my girlfriend here," he says. Skilling—an unassuming, clean-cut 29-year-old—is candid about ECC's appeal. "I completely admit this is geeky," he laughs. "There're several people who come here because they have social-interaction issues; you aren't going to be ridiculed for dressing or acting weird [here]." Stiver has been a part of ECC for seven and a half years. She was introduced to the game when she moved to Seattle after leaving the military. "This is a great outlet for learning to socialize," she says. "I spent the first 22 years of my life without any friends." As the rain drives on, Stiver walks out into the night. She turns back to quote from one of her favorite films, The Lost Boys: "You know what I hate about Santa Carla? All the damn vampires." Stiver turns and walks into the crowd of "fang dorks" as they prepare to crown their new prince of darkness.

||||||||||||||||||||||||||||||||||||||||||||||||||||||||||||||||

WHY ARE ZOMBIES THE NEW BLACK?

COLE ECKHARDT

P ost-apocalyptic pop culture is flooding American televisions and cinemas, and no other trend has escalated in popularity quite like zombie culture.

AMC's nightmarish drama *The Walking Dead* shattered records in the network's ratings this year, according to Time magazine, reaching a viewership of over 28 million. It's really not surprising.

Escapism is what keeps the entertainment industry's moguls in the billionaire's club—but who in their right mind would choose to escape to a shattered society in which all luxury and progress lie trampled beneath hordes of rotting, feral, cannibalistic cadavers?

Zombie culture is just survivalist culture with a trendy aesthetic, and its popularity is revealing this generation's zeitgeist.

Mass-fascination with post-catastrophic conditions is, in part, a subconscious means of preparation, mentally bracing against the anxieties of real, imminent events. The genre reflects all of the crises of overpopulation waiting just around the corner—resource scarcity, systems' collapse and civil unrest on an unprecedented scale—but the problem won't be shambling corpses; it'll be us.

In the words of the scientifically influential, 18th-century cleric Thomas Robert Malthus, "The power of population is so superior to the power of the earth to produce subsistence for man, that premature death must in some shape or other visit the human race. The vices of mankind are active and able ministers of depopulation. They are the precursors in the great army of destruction and often finish the dreadful work themselves. But should they fail in this war of extermination, sickly seasons, epidemics, pestilence and plague advance in terrific array and sweep off their thousands and tens of thousands. Should success be still incomplete, gigantic inevitable famine stalks in the rear and with one mighty blow levels the population."

In just 35 years, if current population-growth trends continue, the UN projects that humanity will be reaching figures over 10 billion, numbers approaching Earth's maximum capacity—resulting in scarcity of fresh water; desertification due to deforestation; air, soil and water contamination irreparably altering the biosphere; rampant poverty leading to devastating crime rates; and microbial pandemics spreading rapidly across what will have become a planetary-scale petri dish.

If any of this sounds familiar, it's because it's a list of every motif from the last decade's worth of end-of-days literature, cinema and television.

But all this still doesn't explain viewers' deep satisfaction in escaping to a hellish world of utter hopelessness.

It's because the circumstances are so humanizing, returning people to a more naturalistic (if at times animalistic) state, reminding them of what truly means anything at all—family, community, love and life itself—and the desperate struggle to protect it all provides audiences with a sort of vicarious fulfillment, assuaging viewers' estrangement from what it meant to be human for hundreds of thousands of years before Xboxes, Pop Tarts, Facebook and Netflix.

But the comforts of modernity could prove to be relatively short-lived. In less than half a century, humanity's very success may be what drags the whole species back into a paradigm of pure survivalism once again, reminding us what being human is really all about.

So enjoy the post-apocalyptic hypotheticals now because when our planet reaches maximum capacity, films like *28 Days Later* will seem like tame, naïve underestimates of the nightmare that's in store for us—that is, if we don't start taking action to prevent such a hell on Earth now.

Discussion Questions

1. What is an "intelligent haunting"? Do you find the evidence for haunted houses (such as the one discussed in Moviepilot) persuasive? Why or why not? How does the author link this event to the cultural phenomenon of gaming?
2. Are ideas about vampires taken seriously in the United States or is this merely a form of popular entertainment? Why do you think these stories are appealing for people?
3. What is the connection between role-playing games and fantasy concerning demonic creatures? What place do such games have in the lives of players?
4. Who are the "real" vampires of New Orleans? How do they mark themselves as a community? How do they see themselves as different from other people? Why does Browning refer to them as a "defiant culture"?
5. Why does Eckhardt believe the popularization of zombies in U.S. culture reveals "this generation's zeitgeist"? Do you agree with him?

Further Readings

1. Kyle William Bishop. *American Zombie Gothic: The Rise and Fall (and Rise) of the Walking Dead in Popular Culture.* Jefferson, NC: McFarland and Company, 2010.
   In this blend of academics and popular writing, literary scholar Bishop explores the world of zombies as a powerful undercurrent in U.S. ideas and fantasy concerning the transcendent, especially in popular culture and cinema. His analysis begins with the slave-era African/Caribbean foundations of the zombie idea and culminates in the post-modern zombie of multiple genres of popular entertainment.

2. Stephanie Boluk and Wylie Lenz, eds. *Generation Zombie: Essays on the Living Dead in Modern Culture*. Jefferson, NC: McFarland and Company, 2011.

   A recent collection of academic essays (mainly from the fields of cultural and media studies) that explore the rise of cinematic and cultural zombies and the living dead as related to a variety of issues, including U.S. imperialism, environmentalism, race, class, and digital technologies.

3. Susannah Clements. *The Vampire Defanged: How the Embodiment of Evil Became a Romantic Hero*. Grand Rapids, MI: Brazos Press, 2011.

   Clements's analysis of the shifting cultural roles of the vampire from monstrous terror through romantic, teenage anti-hero and beyond. Her study may be of special interest to some Christians, as she writes from an explicitly faith-based vantage. Nevertheless, Clements's exploration is a careful, non-polemic one that has particularly strong insight into the historical relationship between Christianity and vampire mythology.

4. Wade Davis. *The Serpent and the Rainbow: A Harvard Scientist's Astonishing Journey into the Secret Societies of Haitian Voodoo, Zombies, and Magic*. New York: Touchstone Books, 1997.

   In this now-classic (though still controversial in some quarters) ethnographic detective story, anthropologist Davis seeks to discover the cultural and pharmacological foundations of the zombie phenomenon in Haiti. Fascinating and extremely well written, the true value of Davis's text lies in its elegant and poignant exploration of the rich tapestry of Haitian Vodou. Not all students of ethnobotany (study of the cultural use of plants) agree with his conclusions, but Davis's study (first published in the early 1980s) had a deep effect on scholarly study of African Caribbean magic and witchcraft that still resonates in the twenty-first century.

5. Mark Collins Jenkins. *Vampire Forensics: Uncovering the Origins of an Enduring Legend*. Washington, DC: National Geographic, 2010. Jenkins's book provides non-specialist readers with a solid introduction to both the cultural and scientific aspects behind vampire beliefs. In particular, his examination of anthropological examples of similar ideas from unrelated social and language groups, and his study of archaeological evidence that in some cases dates back thousands of years, provides an insightful and comprehensive window onto the social functions of vampire myths across human societies.

6. Raymond T. McNally and Radu Florescu. *In Search of Dracula: The History of Dracula and Vampires*. New York: Mariner Books, 1994. This historical biography should be of interest to anyone wishing to understand the foundations of Irish novelist Bram Stoker's fictional character, Count Dracula. In their work, McNally and Florescu document the life and times of fifteenth-century Romanian despot Vlad Tepes III, "son of Dracul," and widely known as "the Impaler." In so doing, the authors' careful analysis of the historical record paints a portrait of the original Dracula that makes his fictional descendent seem rather tame by comparison.

FEAR IN THE WITCHING HOUR

SECTION FIVE
INTRODUCTION

A mong the most popular courses in colleges around the United States are those that delve into the mysterious phenomena of witchcraft. Frequently, such courses are instructed as part of non-specialist general education or introductory-level curricula within departments of anthropology, history, or religious studies. While most students who enroll in these courses have no intention of pursuing careers in these disciplines, the abiding preoccupation among "modern" university students with supernatural forces taken to be sinister or malevolent is a curious fact that demands explanation.

In order to begin this discussion, as with our discussion of magic, we need a definition of our key term, *witchcraft*. Historically, scholars have employed the term witchcraft to refer to transcendent power manipulated by human beings in order to cause harm in the world—most especially by plaguing human beings with misfortune and suffering. This may be direct or indirect action, as in cases where alleged witches create natural disasters or epidemics—these in turn are the source of problems for people. Witchcraft can be analytically distinguished from sorcery on the grounds that the former involves a general belief in the logic of unseen forces while the latter entails such a belief and *also* (typically) secret ritualized activity on the at of a knowledgable agent, or sorcerer.

Because these distinctions are drawn among scholars of witchcraft, the articles in sections five and six explore this enduring fascination from two angles, each of which reflects a distinctive analytical perspective. In this section, the selections have less to do with witchcraft as a type of ritual or religious activity per se, and more to do with an abiding fear of witches and the powers they are said to embody. According to most anthropologists, social historians, and others, it is this fear—and the anxiety it generates—that accounts for the majority of witchcraft beliefs around the world (though not all, as we will see in the next section). As these articles demonstrate, it is the idea of witchcraft, rather than an objective cadre of flesh-and-blood persons and the actions they take, that provokes concern—even in twenty-first-century America. This begs the question of *why*? What is the appeal of witchcraft as a form of explanation, and why, given an abundance of reasoned evidence, do people continue to believe?

Perhaps this question can be partially answered (albeit indirectly) by way of an example. In the United States, much of our cultural fascination with witches and witchcraft can be tied to legal and cultural persecutions that took place in Salem, Massachusetts, in 1692. It is easy to overgeneralize a complex set of events, but the outlines of this episode involved a number of adolescent girls from an initially small number of farming families in Salem Village (modern Danvers) experiencing a variety of physiological symptoms that, by the standards of the time, defied easy medical explanation. These included spontaneous paralysis, visions, glossolalia (speaking in tongues), and animal mimicry. In the absence of medical explanation, Salem residents (chief among them the community pastor) proposed that a conspiracy of Satan-inspired witches lay at the heart of the girls' torment. Over the spring and summer months of 1692, an ever-widening circle of "witches" were arrested. All of these, oddly enough, either fit a well-established profile of what witches were said to be like, or were at odds with the victims' families, the Salem pastor, and his allies. Of these, over twenty ultimately died—most were hanged, but one man was tortured to death and several others died in prison awaiting trial.

These, then, are the general circumstances surrounding the persecutions. Social historians have long suspected that, whatever the views of Salem residents, explanation for the episode could be found not so much in the diabolical, but in the entanglement of social and cultural forces. Whereas the earliest English residents of the Massachusetts colony are believed to have shared a general vision of New England as a "promised land" in which a new kingdom of God on earth might be erected, by the late seventeenth century such expectations had been eroded by an expanding and increasingly diverse population. For some, namely those urbanized individuals and families involved in trade, shipbuilding, and pub keeping (to mention but a few), the experience of colonial life had paid fat dividends. For others, especially the agrarian farming class, early expectations of a land of plenty and prosperity had given way to a grim reality of shrinking land holdings and decreased profits. Historical research on the Salem trials suggests that the accusers and accused tended to fall on either side of this socioeconomic line: accusers tended to be the children of downtrodden, embittered farming families, while those accused tended to be either the relatively affluent residents of port towns or traditional social outcasts (targeted for racial background or allegedly immoral conduct). Still others among the accused had been involved in interpersonal disputes with the families of the afflicted. Add to this deep anxieties about conflicts with Native Americans, fear of contagious disease, and unease about the future political independence of the colony, and the proverbial table is set for rampant scapegoating: in all cases, those accused at Salem may be thought of as convenient targets for malaise and anger that had few, if any, other outlets. Whatever their real historical foundations, the 1692 persecutions remain an enigma in the public imagination. Many continue to ask such questions as, Who were the witches? Were they real? Were innocents targeted? Did the devil really live in Salem? Does the devil continue to plague our society today?

For the anthropologist of modern popular culture, the continuing popularity of Satan worship—and the alleged witchcraft it provokes— as a narrative that explains misfortune is at least as interesting as questions about the objective reality of witches. If we strongly suspect that witchcraft accusations are one outcome of complex and troubling social and cultural circumstances, as the Salem events suggest, then why do such explanations continue to have power over the public imagination? Though diverse in their origins and assumptions, the articles in section five have in common the idea that modern allegations of witchcraft are being made by a wide variety of people addressing a range of social, economic, medical, and ecological misfortunes. Reading between the lines, these articles illustrate how witchcraft fears tend to arise in social environments of severe stress in which there seem to be no immediate explanations or resolutions. In circumstances of extreme hardship—such as those brought on by famine, drought, epidemic, or warfare—most, if not all, cultural systems of meaning provide ways of accounting for and symbolically resolving endemic and destructive problems (that is, by identifying and punishing those responsible).

Specifically, let us consider the article on Vodou (or Voodoo), which touches on religious tradition in Haiti. It is included to show just how far this much-misunderstood and -maligned religious tradition has to go in order to transcend its many associations with witchcraft and evil— ideas that are themselves deeply rooted in the European American experience as a form of racism that charges so-called primitive peoples with unevolved motives and practices. In the wake of the calamitous earthquake in early 2010, reports in the mainstream media concerning vibrant "prayer in the streets" and the general "faithful" character of the Haitian people carefully avoided mention (intentionally or not) of Vodou as the religion in question; only in later months would decidedly uncharitable editorials surface suggesting that those same people who had suffered so greatly were at least partially responsible for their own plight, having clung against all reason to the Vodou traditions that many U.S. evangelicals and others styled as superstitious, if not outright Satanic. It is hard to escape the conclusion that assumptions are being made about the intrinsically violent and malevolent character of Vodou itself, which many anthropologists have written extensively about as a beautiful, peaceful, and theologically rich tradition.

However, the impact of these articles is paradoxical, because they do more than merely describe events or religious practices; in giving voice to such beliefs, such discussions tend to lend credence to witchcraft as a form of explanation even when their authors don't intend for them to do so. A faint, if inconsistent, pattern is thus discernable among these and the other reports included in this section. On one hand, reports of witchcraft "pogroms" in central Africa and Haiti lend weight to widespread, often racialized assumptions about the "rational" world in which allegedly modern (and manifestly white) Americans live. We, modern Americans, are thus better than "primitives" who still believe in the power of witchcraft. It is as if to say that these things happened 300 years ago among us (at Salem) but they could never happen now—as a society, we are evolved, mature, and "disenchanted" (to use a term popular among historians). In the modern world, the implication is that such superstitions are relegated to various forms of popular entertainment—television, movies, fiction, electronic games, and so on.

On the other hand, such reports have a second, no less significant effect: they feed an enduring, if mostly unspoken uncertainty about what really happened at Salem and what really happens in the world today. For many people, religion is serious business—the Bible and clergy speak of demons and witchcraft, so on what grounds should these stories be dismissed? When a voodoo priestess is forced to defend herself against allegations that a technical snafu during the Superbowl was caused by witchcraft, the effect is no doubt comical for many. But for others, a suspicion lingers—is Satanic witchcraft a real phenomenon, and consequently a logical explanation for unfortunate events, great and small?

Coming at this issue from a different angle, we may also approach the study of witchcraft in the non-Western world from the vantage of globalization, in that the spread of Western lifeways, religious traditions, and economies has tended to foster both socioeconomic malaise and expectations of malevolent sorcery. There is, in fact, little evidence in Africa for the "European-style" witch hunt prior to that region's contact with Western society and the religious traditions it brought. To the contrary, classic examples from anthropology show that although believed to be common, witchcraft in, for instance, the southern Sudan was traditionally viewed as an inherited organic defect that combined with negative emotion to create misfortune for individuals on the receiving end of enmity. Frequently, witches never even realized their capacity to inflict harm any more than a carrier of the flu virus realizes they are passing it along to people who they come in contact with. It is this benign history that makes current events—such as children being brutally murdered by raging mobs determined to root out the sources of misfortune in their midst—all the more tragic. In Europe, the Mediterranean, the Middle East, and European North America, by contrast, witches have long been linked to the workings of un-Godly malevolence, and have been targeted as Satan's accomplices. Their extirpation—through punishment of varying degrees of severity—provides the basis of social recovery and renewed prosperity, much as the eradication of cancer cells leads to renewed health of an organism.

The stubborn persistence of such a vision should not be underestimated, even in regards to an organization as complex and "rational" as the modern Roman Catholic Church. Over the past several generations (and contrary to what many have believed), the upper hierarchies of Catholicism have been defenders of science and academic rigor against the various magic-driven logics and fundamentalisms of global Christianity. However, this has not meant that the Church has altogether abandoned what some would consider the medieval reasoning that haunted theology in earlier times. Feeding on a wide range of modern fears and anxieties, some within the Church hierarchy call for a renewed attention to traditional explanations of, and even methods for dealing with Satanism and the worldly evils said to flow from it. In many cases, allegations of diabolical influence would seem to be directed at rank-and-file Catholics who dabble in unorthodox or unsanctioned forms of religious experience and activity (for instance, the experience of supernaturally powerful visions, however holy their focus). In others, some within the Church allege the deliberate and conspiratorial actions of Satanists whose chief goal remains to undermine God's plan for the world and the Church. To the end of combatting this rising tide, some even call for an increase in numbers of Catholic clergy trained in supernatural warfare, or exorcism.

It is perhaps this general, ongoing concern that is the foundation of real world fears concerning such otherwise entertaining figures whose adventures are recounted in J.K. Rowling's *Harry Potter* novels and the massively popular film franchise they inspired. The Devil, it seems, finds many points of entry into human life. Neither has mass social media been immune to diabolical infiltration, as accusations of witchcraft have, in at least one case, had the most sobering consequences imaginable.

Although the articles in this section represent only a narrow sliver of media reportage concerning perceptions of witchcraft in the modern world, they suffice to give readers a sense of the range of the contradictions and inconsistencies embedded in witchcraft as a form of cultural explanation. Unfortunately, it is equally clear that in the twenty-first century, the idea of witchcraft remains popular and compelling for many around the world, and that new media technologies do not so much discourage or dispel such beliefs as encourage, spread, and even normalize them. Even in the halls of the U.S. Capitol, as late as 2014 the specter of witchcraft was floated by a conservative bishop as part of a prayer for the nation. America, Bishop Angel Nunez claimed, risked losing God's divine protection if such devilry wasn't eliminated. In considering carefully the various fears and perspectives enlivening such rhetoric, readers might use the unusual events described in these articles as a lens through which to better understand how we think about others who are somehow different from us—physically, culturally, and morally.

|||||||||||||||||||||||||||||||||||||||||||||||||||||||||||||||||||||||||

MOB KILLS WITCHCRAFT COUPLE

BONGANI HANS

A woman and her husband were burnt to death in Pietermaritzburg on Wednesday afternoon after they were accused of having abducted a 7-year-old boy to use for witchcraft.

Tholakele Shoba, 54, a trainee traditional healer, and her husband Shezi, 60, were killed in Snathing near Edendale at about 13:00.

About 100 community members who killed them sat next to the bodies until a mortuary van collected their badly burnt bodies at about 18:30.

Boy's Body Found

The community members repeatedly said the couple deserved to die in that way because they had abducted a number of people who are still missing. The couple's house was also set alight.

The attack followed the disappearance of 11-year-old Mthokozisi Mpanza on November 11. His body was discovered on November 17 in a nearby stream with body parts missing. He was buried on Sunday.

The community members went to a sangoma—known only as Ngcobo—on Wednesday morning and he told them that Shoba had abducted the child.

It is alleged that he told them the body they had found was not that of a real human being, but had been created through muthi.

A community member who declined to be named told *The Witness*: "He told us that Mthokozisi was still alive and that maShoba has kept him together with other locals, who were also abducted. When we returned from Ngcobo we called a meeting at our traditional leader's house to give them the feedback. We then asked maShoba to tell us where she kept the child.

"Shoba was summoned from town by telephone, and came to the meeting little suspecting what was going to happen."

Admitted Kidnapping Boy

"After interrogating her, she admitted that she kidnapped the boy and told us that she used him for witchcraft purposes.

"Her husband started to hit people, which provoked people to attack them with sticks and stones before they set them alight," said the community member.

Mthokozisi's 25-year-old sister said they believed what Ngcobo had told them.

"That Ngcobo is a credible sangoma, who is well-trained. He even showed us his certificates. We had no reason not to believe what he told us. He said he can even stand in court to defend what he told us," said the sister.

Shoba's elder brother, Gugu Shoba, 55, said he was shocked at the way his sister and brother-in-law were killed.

"They did not have to burn them. At least they should just have killed them."

"Usually is it true what the sangomas foresee, although I cannot say my sister was guilty of practising witchcraft," said Shoba.

The couple had a 10-year-old boy living with them. He arrived home from school to find their house burning.

Police spokesperson Warrant Officer Joey Jeevan said no one has been arrested.

She was not in a position to say whether the sangoma will be arrested as an accessory to murder.

"Police are investigating the matter," said Jeevan.

AFRICAN CHILDREN DENOUNCED AS WITCHES BY CHRISTIAN PASTORS

KATHARINE HOURELD

The nine-year-old boy lay on a bloodstained hospital sheet crawling with ants, staring blindly at the wall.

His family pastor had accused him of being a witch, and his father then tried to force acid down his throat as an exorcism. It spilled as he struggled, burning away his face and eyes. The emaciated boy barely had strength left to whisper the name of the church that had denounced him—Mount Zion Lighthouse.

A month later, he died.

Nwanaokwo Edet was one of an increasing number of children in Africa accused of witchcraft by pastors and then tortured or killed, often by family members. Pastors were involved in half of 200 cases of "witch children" reviewed by the AP, and 13 churches were named in the case files.

Some of the churches involved are renegade local branches of international franchises. Their parishioners take literally the Biblical exhortation, "Thou shalt not suffer a witch to live."

"It is an outrage what they are allowing to take place in the name of Christianity," said Gary Foxcroft, head of nonprofit Stepping Stones Nigeria.

For their part, the families are often extremely poor, and sometimes even relieved to have one less mouth to feed. Poverty, conflict, and poor education lay the foundation for accusations, which are then triggered by the death of a relative, the loss of a job or the denunciation of a pastor on the make, said Martin Dawes, a spokesman for the United Nations Children's Fund.

"When communities come under pressure, they look for scapegoats," he said. "It plays into traditional beliefs that someone is responsible for a negative change … and children are defenseless."

The idea of witchcraft is hardly new, but it has taken on new life recently partly because of a rapid growth in evangelical Christianity. Campaigners against the practice say around 15,000 children have been accused in two of Nigeria's 36 states over the past decade and around 1,000 have been murdered. In the past month alone, three Nigerian children accused of witchcraft were killed and another three were set on fire.

Nigeria is one of the heartlands of abuse, but hardly the only one: the United Nations Children's Fund says tens of thousands of children have been targeted throughout Africa.

Church signs sprout around every twist of the road snaking through the jungle between Uyo, the capital of the southern Akwa Ibom state where Nwanaokwo lay, and Eket, home to many more rejected "witch children." Churches outnumber schools, clinics and banks put together. Many promise to solve parishioner's material worries as well as spiritual ones—eight out of ten Nigerians struggle by on less than $2 a day.

"Poverty must catch fire," insists the Born 2 Rule Crusade on one of Uyo's main streets.

"Where little shots become big shots in a short time," promises the Winner's Chapel down the road.

"Pray your way to riches," advises Embassy of Christ a few blocks away.

It's hard for churches to carve out a congregation with so much competition. So some pastors establish their credentials by accusing children of witchcraft.

Nwanaokwo said he knew the pastor who accused him only as Pastor King. Mount Zion Lighthouse in Nigeria at first confirmed that a Pastor King worked for them, then denied that they knew any such person.

Bishop A.D. Ayakndue, the head of the church in Nigeria, said pastors were encouraged to pray about witchcraft, but not to abuse children.

"We pray over that problem (of witchcraft) very powerfully," he said. "But we can never hurt a child."

The Nigerian church is a branch of a Californian church by the same name. But the California church says it lost touch with its Nigerian offshoots several years ago.

"I had no idea," said church elder Carrie King by phone from Tracy, Calif. "I knew people believed in witchcraft over there but we believe in the power of prayer, not physically harming people."

The Mount Zion Lighthouse—also named by three other families as the accuser of their children—is part of the powerful Pentecostal Fellowship of Nigeria. The Fellowship's president, Ayo Oritsejafor, said the Fellowship was the fastest-growing religious group in Nigeria, with more than 30 million members.

"We have grown so much in the past few years we cannot keep an eye on everybody," he explained.

But Foxcroft, the head of Stepping Stones, said if the organization was able to collect membership fees, it could also police its members better. He had already written to the organization twice to alert it to the abuse, he said. He suggested the fellowship ask members to sign forms denouncing abuse or hold meetings to educate pastors about the new child rights law in the state of Akwa Ibom, which makes it illegal to denounce children as witches. Similar laws and education were needed in other states, he said.

Sam Itauma of the Children's Rights and Rehabilitation Network said it is the most vulnerable children—the orphaned, sick, disabled or poor—who are most often denounced. In Nwanaokwo's case, his poor father and dead mother made him an easy target.

"Even churches who didn't use to 'find' child witches are being forced into it by the competition," said Itauma. "They are seen as spiritually powerful because they can detect witchcraft and the parents may even pay them money for an exorcism."

That's what Margaret Eyekang did when her 8-year-old daughter Abigail was accused by a "prophet" from the Apostolic Church, because the girl liked to sleep outside on hot nights—interpreted as meaning she might be flying off to join a coven. A series of exorcisms cost Eyekang eight months' wages, or US$270. The payments bankrupted her.

Neighbors also attacked her daughter.

"They beat her with sticks and asked me why I was bringing them a witch child," she said. A relative offered Eyekang floor space but Abigail was not welcome and had to sleep in the streets.

Members of two other families said pastors from the Apostolic Church had accused their children of witchcraft, but asked not to be named for fear of retaliation.

The Nigeria Apostolic Church refused repeated requests made by phone, email and in person for comment.

At first glance, there's nothing unusual about the laughing, grubby kids playing hopscotch or reading from a tattered Dick and Jane book by the graffiti-scrawled cinderblock house. But this is where children like Abigail end up after being labeled witches by churches and abandoned or tortured by their families.

There's a scar above Jane's shy smile: her mother tried to saw off the top of her skull after a pastor denounced her and repeated exorcisms costing a total of $60 didn't cure her of witchcraft. Mary, 15, is just beginning to think about boys and how they will look at the scar tissue on her face caused when her mother doused her in caustic soda. Twelve-year-old Rachel dreamed of being a banker but instead was chained up by her pastor, starved and beaten with sticks repeatedly; her uncle paid him $60 for the exorcism.

Israel's cousin tried to bury him alive, Nwaekwa's father drove a nail through her head, and sweet-tempered Jerry—all knees, elbows and toothy grin—was beaten by his pastor, starved, made to eat cement and then set on fire by his father as his pastor's wife cheered it on.

The children at the home run by Itauma's organization have been mutilated as casually as the praying mantises they play with. Home officials asked for the children's last names not to be used to protect them from retaliation.

The home was founded in 2003 with seven children; it now has 120 to 200 at any given time as children are reconciled with their families and new victims arrive.

Helen Ukpabio is one of the few evangelists publicly linked to the denunciation of child witches. She heads the enormous Liberty Gospel church in Calabar, where Nwanaokwo used to live. Ukpabio makes and distributes popular books and DVDs on witchcraft; in one film, a group of child witches pull out a man's eyeballs. In another book, she advises that 60 percent of the inability to bear children is caused by witchcraft.

In an interview with the AP, Ukpabio is accompanied by her lawyer, church officials and personal film crew.

"Witchcraft is real," Ukpabio insisted, before denouncing the physical abuse of children. Ukpabio says she performs non-abusive exorcisms for free and was not aware of or responsible for any misinterpretation of her materials.

"I don't know about that," she declared.

However, she then acknowledged that she had seen a pastor from the Apostolic Church break a girl's jaw during an exorcism. Ukpabio said she prayed over her that night and cast out the demon. She did not respond to questions on whether she took the girl to hospital or complained about the injury to church authorities.

After activists publicly identified Liberty Gospel as denouncing "child witches," armed police arrived at Itauma's home accompanied by a church lawyer. Three children were injured in the fracas. Itauma asked that other churches identified by children not be named to protect their victims.

"We cannot afford to make enemies of all the churches around here," he said. "But we know the vast majority of them are involved in the abuse even if their headquarters aren't aware."

Just mentioning the name of a church is enough to frighten a group of bubbly children at the home.

"Please stop the pastors who hurt us," said Jerry quietly, touching the scars on his face. "I believe in God and God knows I am not a witch."

MOBS LYNCH WITCHES IN HAITI FOR SPREADING CHOLERA EPIDEMIC

THE SYDNEY MORNING HERALD

Haitian mobs fearing a cholera epidemic have killed people whom they had accused of trying to spread the disease, including through witchcraft, police say.

"A dozen people accused of importing cholera to a region that so far has been spared were killed with machetes and stones and their corpses were burned in the streets," a police inspector said.

A prosecutor, Kesner Numa, said, "These people are accused of witchcraft related to cholera." The attackers believed the victims were trying to "plant a substance that spreads the disease in the region."

The first lynching cases took place last week. "Since then we have had cases every day," the prosecutor said.

Communities in the Grand Anse region in the far south-west of Haiti were refusing to co-operate with investigations into the killings.

"They really believe that witches are taking advantage of the cholera epidemic to kill." It was not immediately clear if any of the victims had cholera.

Six people were hacked or stoned to death in the town of Chambellan and five others in Marfranc and Dame Marie, officials said.

According to journalists, at least three people were killed by mobs in the city of Jeremie, while several others were killed under similar circumstances in surrounding villages.

Health authorities say Grand Anse is the region least affected by the cholera epidemic, which has killed 1817 in Haiti since mid-October. Only five of those deaths have been reported in Grand Anse.

About half of Haiti's population is believed to practise the voodoo religion in some form, although many are thought to also follow other religious beliefs at the same time.

||||||||||||||||||||||||||||||||||||||||||||||||||||||||

CATHOLIC BISHOPS

ARTICLE 24

More Exorcists Needed

RACHEL ZOLL

C iting a shortage of priests who can perform the rite, the nation's Roman Catholic bishops are holding a conference on how to conduct exorcisms.

The two-day training, which ends Saturday in Baltimore, is to outline the scriptural basis of evil, instruct clergy on evaluating whether a person is truly possessed, and review the prayers and rituals that comprise an exorcism. Among the speakers will be Cardinal Daniel DiNardo, archbishop of Galveston-Houston, Texas, and a priest-assistant to New York Archbishop Timothy Dolan.

"Learning the liturgical rite is not difficult," DiNardo said in a phone interview before the conference, which is open to clergy only. "The problem is the discernment that the exorcist needs before he would ever attempt the rite."

More than 50 bishops and 60 priests signed up to attend, according to Catholic News Service, which first reported the event. The conference was scheduled for just ahead of the fall meeting of the U.S. Conference of Catholic Bishops, which starts Monday in Baltimore.

Despite strong interest in the training, skepticism about the rite persists within the American church. Organizers of the event are keenly aware of the ridicule that can accompany discussion of the subject. Exorcists in U.S. dioceses keep a very low profile. In 1999, the church updated the Rite of Exorcism, cautioning that "all must be done to avoid the perception that exorcism is magic or superstition."

The practice is much more accepted by Catholics in parts of Europe and elsewhere overseas. Cardinal Stanislaw Dziwisz, the longtime private secretary of Pope John Paul II, revealed a few years after the pontiff's death that John Paul had performed an exorcism on a woman who was brought into the Vatican writhing and screaming in what Dziwisz said was a case of possession by the devil.

Bishop Thomas Paprocki of Springfield, Ill., who organized the conference, said only a tiny number of U.S. priests have enough training and knowledge to perform an exorcism. Dioceses nationwide have been relying solely on these clergy, who have been overwhelmed with requests to evaluate claims. The Rev. James LeBar, who was the official exorcist of the Archdiocese of New York under the late Cardinal John O'Connor, had faced a similar level of demand, traveling the country in response to the many requests for his expertise.

The rite is performed only rarely. Neal Lozano, a Catholic writer and author of the book *Unbound: A Practical Guide to Deliverance* about combatting evil spirits, said he knows an exorcist in the church who receives about 400 inquiries a year, but determines that out of that number, two or three of the cases require an exorcism.

No one knows why more people seem to be seeking the rite. Paprocki said one reason could be the growing interest among Americans in exploring general spirituality, as opposed to participating in organized religion, which has led more people to dabble in the occult.

"They don't know exactly what they're getting into and when they have questions, they're turning to the church, to priests," said Paprocki, chairman of the bishops' committee on canonical affairs and church governance. "They wonder if some untoward activity is taking place in their life and want some help discerning that."

Many Catholic immigrants in the U.S. come from countries where exorcism is more common, although Paprocki said that was not a motivation for organizing the conference.

Exorcism has deep roots in Christianity. The New Testament contains several examples of Jesus casting out evil spirits from people, and the church notes these acts in the Catholic Catechism. Whether or not individual Catholics realize it, each of them undergoes what the church calls a minor exorcism at baptism that includes prayers renouncing Satan and seeking freedom from original sin.

A major exorcism can only be performed by a priest with the permission of his bishop after a thorough evaluation, including consulting with physicians or psychiatrists to rule out any psychological or physical illness behind the person's behavior.

Signs of demonic possession accepted by the church include violent reaction to holy water or anything holy, speaking in a language the possessed person doesn't know and abnormal displays of strength.

The full exorcism is held in private and includes sprinkling holy water, reciting Psalms, reading aloud from the Gospel, laying on of hands and reciting the Lord's Prayer. Some adaptations are allowed for different circumstances. The exorcist can invoke the Holy Spirit then blow in the face of the possessed person, trace the sign of the cross on the person's forehead and command the devil to leave.

The training comes at a time when many American bishops and priests are trying to correct what they view as a lack of emphasis on the Catholic teaching about sin and evil after the Second Vatican Council, the series of meetings in the 1960s that enacted modernizing reforms in the church. Many in the American hierarchy, as well as Pope Benedict XVI, believe that the supernatural aspect of the church was lost in the changes, reducing it to just another institution in the world.

A renewed focus on exorcism highlights the divine element of the church and underscores the belief that evil is real.

DiNardo said some Catholics who ask for an exorcism are really seeking, "prayerful support. They're asking for formation in the faith." Still, he said sometimes the rite is warranted.

"For the longest time, we in the United States may not have been as much attuned to some of the spiritual aspects of evil because we have become so much attached to what would be either physical or psychological explanation for certain phenomena," DiNardo said. "We may have forgotten that there is a spiritual dimension to people."

||||||||||||||||||||||||||||||||||||||||||||||||||||||||||

VATICAN DENOUNCES GROUP'S CLAIM OF SEEING THE VIRGIN MARY MORE THAN 40,000 TIMES AS "WORK OF THE DEVIL"

DAILY MAIL ONLINE

The Vatican has denounced a group who claim to have seen the Virgin Mary more than 40,000 times in the past 27 years.

The six Bosnian "seers" attract five million pilgrims a year to their home town of Medjugorje, providing a lucrative trade for local businesses.

Hundreds of thousands travel there each year from Britain alone.

The Vatican has rejected claims made by the six Bosnian "seers" that they have seen the Virgin Mary more than 40,000 times over the past 27 years.

But now one of the most respected voices in the Roman Catholic church has accused the visionaries of perpetuating a "diabolical deceit."

Andrea Gemma, 77, a bishop and once the Vatican's top exorcist, told a magazine in Italy, "In Medjugorje everything happens in function of money: pilgrimages, lodging houses, sale of trinkets.

"This whole sham is the work of the Devil. It is a scandal.'"He said the Vatican would soon crack down on the group.

The Medjugorje phenomenon began on June 25, 1981, when six children told a priest they had seen the Virgin on a hillside near their town.

A church investigation dismissed the vision, and the Vatican banned pilgrimages to the site in 1985. But many Catholics ignored the ban.

Today, the seers own smart houses with security gates and tennis courts and expensive cars. One is married to a former U.S. beauty queen.

Catholic officials in the U.S. have recently banned the group from speaking on church property during their world tours, on which they allegedly take the Virgin with them.

BLOOD OF POPE JOHN PAUL II STOLEN IN POSSIBLE "SATANIC" THEFT

ARTICLE 26

NICK SQUIRES

A religious reliquary containing blood from the late Pope John Paul II has been stolen from a remote mountain church in Italy, with speculation that a Satanic group could be behind the theft.

A team of around 50 Carabinieri police officers with sniffer dogs were on Monday searching for any trace of the reliquary, which was stolen from the Church of St Peter of Ienca in the Abruzzo mountains at the weekend.

The ornate gold object contains a fragment of material, stained with blood, which was purportedly taken from the clothing worn by John Paul II after he was shot during the failed attempt on his life in St Peter's Square in 1981.

It was donated to the church in May 2011 by Stanislaw Dzuwisz, a Polish cardinal and the Pope's former personal secretary.

The reliquary is one of just a handful in the world that contains the blood of the Polish pope, who died in 2005 and was succeeded by Benedict XVI.

It was stolen along with a cross from the church, which lies close to Gran Sasso, a 9,550 ft- high mountain in the Apennines east of Rome.

The theft was discovered on Saturday by a priest from the religious sanctuary, which is dedicated to the memory of John Paul II.

The Pope was very fond of the region and used to spend holidays there, walking, meditating and skiing at the nearby resort of Campo Imperatore.

It is also famous as the place where Benito Mussolini was interned after Italy swapped sides during the war, and from where he was rescued by a team of German paratroopers in September 1943 during a daring airborne raid.

"It's possible that there could be Satanic sects behind the theft of the reliquary," said Giovanni Panunzio, the national coordinator of an anti-occult group called Osservatorio Antiplagio.

"This period of the year is important in the Satanic calendar and culminates in the Satanic 'new year' on February 1. This sort of sacrilege often takes place at this time of the year. We hope that the stolen items are recovered as quickly as possible."

The theft of the reliquary comes as the Vatican prepares to canonize John Paul II, along with another former Pope, John XXIII, at a ceremony on April 27.

At John Paul II's funeral in 2005, crowds of mourners cried "Santo Subito!"—"Sainthood now"—prompting the Vatican to speed up the Polish pontiff's path to canonisation.

In Aug. 2012, another relic containing a vial of the late Pope's blood was stolen from a Catholic priest while he was travelling on a train north of Rome.

The relic was in his backpack, which was swiped by thieves but later recovered in a thicket of cane grass by police.

IS HARRY POTTER IN CAHOOTS WITH HELL?

Hit Movie Renews Concerns that Children Are Being Lured to Satan

DREW ZAHN

ARTICLE 27

F or the second weekend in a row, *Harry Potter and the Deathly Hallows: Part 1*—the seventh film in author J.K. Rowling's fantastically successful series about young wizards—sits atop the box office charts, smashing ticket-sale records as the franchise only gains steam en route to its finale.

But the wild success of "Pottermania" has also brought back critics of the franchise who question—or even outright condemn—the movies' spiritual ramifications.

"*Harry Potter* and these *Twilight* vampires glamorize the power of evil," argues author and Roman Catholic Priest Thomas J. Euteneuers.

A practicing exorcist, Euteneuers told Deal W. Hudson of InsideCatholic that he intended his new book, *Exorcism and the Church Militant*, as a warning on how the *Harry Potter* series and Stephenie Meyer's *Twilight* movies about teenage vampires, for example, desensitize children to "the dark world" of witchcraft.

Euteneuers says the wild popularity of the *Potter* films encourages children and teens to be curious, even to dabble in occult activity, trying their own hands at magic spells, tarot cards, Ouija boards and the like. And once kids start "playing around" with the occult, he says, it "opens a window" for Satan and his minions.

"Demons do not discriminate between intentions—no matter how innocent—and children lose the clear distinction between good and evil," Euteneuers says. "This has led to many, many cases of [demon] possession among young people."

In fact, a Barna Research Group study conducted in 2002 discovered that 12 percent of teens surveyed said they were more interested in witchcraft as a result of watching the *Potter* films and reading Rowling's books.

But does that additional interest really turn into demonic possession?

Euteneuers is far from the first to question the effects of Pottermania, as the series has been haunted by criticism and calls for caution since *Harry Potter* first became popular more than a decade ago.

As WND reported, the Vatican's top exorcist has condemned J.K. Rowling's best-selling *Harry Potter* series as leading children to the devil.

Rev. Gabriele Amorth said, "You start off with Harry Potter, who comes across as a likeable wizard, but you end up with the devil. There is no doubt that the signature of the Prince of Darkness is clearly within these books."

Amorth made similar comments back in 2002 and suggested children are drawn to the occult by the novels.

"By reading *Harry Potter*, a young child will be drawn into magic and from there it is a simple step to Satanism and the devil," he said.

Harry Potter's creator, J.K. Rowling, has repeatedly denied that her books lead children to the occult.

"I absolutely did not start writing these books to encourage any child into witchcraft," Rowling told CNN in a 1999 interview. "I'm laughing slightly because to me, the idea is absurd. I have met thousands of children and not even one time has a child come up to me and said, 'Ms. Rowling, I'm so glad I've read these books because now I want to be a witch.'"

Nonetheless, the debate continues over how the wizards of *Potter's* world affect children of this world.

"My greatest concern is that godly fear that protects mankind from dabbling in the spirit world is being taken away from children who read these *Harry Potter* books," says filmmaker and occult expert Caryl Matrisciana, producer of the documentary *Harry Potter: Witchcraft Repackaged*.

"The terrors and horrors of black magic and occult practice, rituals, ceremonies and demon possession are being normalized," she said. "Alarmingly, the *Potter* books are engaging in pagan discipleship, disciplining our children to spiritual alternatives and also turning them away from the biblical principles and God's protection."

Others argue that the *Potter* series is merely harmless fantasy.

"I don't think there's anyone in this room who grew up without fairies, magic, and angels in their imaginary world," Rev. Peter Fleetwood, a former official of the Pontifical Council for Culture, says. "They aren't bad. They aren't serving as an anti-Christian ideology."

Jack Brock, pastor of Christ Community Church in Alamogordo, N.M., known for actually burning Rowling's books in 2001, disagrees, saying there's an important distinction between Harry Potter and the witches in *Snow White* or *The Wizard of Oz*.

"The difference is that in *Snow White and the Seven Dwarfs*, Snow White is the heroine," Brock said. "In *The Wizard of Oz*, Dorothy is the heroine and the wizard turned out to be a con man. … In *Harry Potter*, Harry is the hero and he is a witch. That is a big crossover there in their approach."

In his review of the fourth *Harry Potter* movie, film critic and chairman of the Christian Film & Television Commission Dr. Ted Baehr agreed:

"Although it may be argued that the *Harry Potter* books and movies are just fantasy stories having nothing to do with reality, they still entice impressionable young children, teenagers, and even adults with an elitist worldview full of occultism and paganism," he writes. "This fact is clearly demonstrated by the movie's story, where Harry not only uses witchcraft to defeat evil and to gain happiness, but also consults with the ghosts of his dead parents. This fact is further demonstrated by the publisher and film studio websites for young fans of the series, where children can experiment with witchcraft and even worship pagan Gods. If Harry Potter is so innocent, why do these evil, heretical websites exist?"

With only one movie left to be released in the 8-film franchise, a movie in which— *spoiler alert!* —young Harry will follow a path very similar to the one followed by Jesus of Nazareth nearly 2,000 years ago, the debate over *Harry Potter's* religious ramifications is apparently far from over.

WOMAN BEATEN TO DEATH AFTER BEING ACCUSED OF WITCHCRAFT ON FACEBOOK

ANNALEE NEWITZ

At last Facebook has brought us back to the middle ages, just as we knew it would. A woman in the Brazilian city Guarujá, near São Paolo, was beaten to death last week after Facebook rumors circulated that she was a witch.

A local news outlet, Guarujá Alerta, posted a rumor on its Facebook page that Fabiane Maria de Jesus was kidnapping children for black magic rituals. They included a picture of the woman, who was subsequently beaten to death by people who had read about her online. One of them even filmed the beating.

De Jesus was a housewife in her early thirties, and police say she has no criminal record and has not ever been reported for kidnapping. Guarujá Alerta has taken down the post about her from their Facebook page, but page administrators told the Brazilian newspaper *Folha de São Paulo* that they were merely passing along the story as a "rumor" and that they couldn't be held responsible.

This is just an extreme example of how the social relationships made possible online are in many ways the same as the old ones. Rumors on Facebook can result in a lynching—just the way rumors in villages resulted in lynchings during the Inquisition. If you're still convinced that social media will create a more beautiful and egalitarian future for humanity, just remember that the wisdom of crowds sometimes ends in the public beating of an innocent woman for witchcraft.

Discussion Questions

1. How have those accused of witchcraft been treated in Africa and Haiti? How do such accusations in these areas help to offset fears and anxieties cause by social, economic, political, and environmental problems?
2. What are the social and theological reasons behind a resurgence of interest in exorcism within the Roman Catholic Church? Generally, why does the Roman Catholic Church denounce some beliefs and practices as the work of the Devil or his Satanic human agents?
3. Why do some people believe the *Harry Potter* phenomenon to be a work of the Devil? What is the logic behind such arguments? Do you believe them? Why or why not?
4. According to the article, what was the basis for rumors about a Brazilian woman on Facebook? What was the result? How do you think such situations might be avoided in the future?

Further Readings

1. Emerson W. Baker. *A Storm of Witchcraft: The Salem Trials and the American Experience.* Oxford University Press, 2014.
   This acclaimed book places the events of the 1692 witchcraft persecutions in the wider context of social, political, and religious developments in New England and Great Britain, and examines the legacy of the Salem trials in U.S. public memory.
2. Leslie G. Desmangles. *The Faces of the Gods: Vodou and Roman Catholicism in Haiti.* Chapel Hill, NC: University of North Carolina Press, 1992.
   Written for students of anthropology and other scholars, this is perhaps the most comprehensive ethnographic study of the Vodou religion in Haiti. Desmangles is especially adept at deciphering the

tangled relationship between the Western African spirit beliefs (the cultural foundations of Vodou) and the seventeenth- and eighteenth-century European Catholicism that provided a ritual framework for a syncretism that remains central to Haitian religion today.

3. E. E. Evans-Pritchard. *Witchcraft, Oracles, and Magic Among the Azande*, Abridged Edition. Oxford University Press, 1976.

Perhaps the best known ethnographic study of witchcraft beliefs in a non-European setting. Although at times made dense by Evans-Pritchard's 1930s-era prose and by the details of structural-functionalist theory, the abridged version of this work remains seminal and relevant today. It is especially important for anyone wishing to understand how witchcraft beliefs (explicitly opposed to actual practice in Evans-Pritchard's formulation) can be interpreted as motivating individuals to follows social norms and conventions, and functioning to ensure social order and integration.

4. Felicitas D. Goodman. *How About Demons? Possession and Exorcism in the Modern World.* Bloomington and Indianapolis, IN: Indiana University Press, 1988.

This 1980s book on the folklore and anthropology of possession and exorcism remains one of the few cross-cultural studies available on the topic. Drawing on ethnographic examples from Japan, Brazil, Mexico, Africa, and popular U.S. culture, Goodman (a professional folklorist and Ursuline nun) explores the phenomenon from the perspective of desiring to understand the role of trance and possession states in human culture.

5. Karen Palmer. *Spellbound: Inside West Africa's Witch Camps.* New York: Free Press, 2010.

Palmer is a journalist who writes with deep compassion about northern Ghana's disturbing phenomenon of "witch camps." These squalid communities are a refuge for women accused of witchcraft who are forced to leave their families, homes, and communities. Palmer's study focuses on popular belief in witchcraft as the source of profound misfortune and illness, as well as on the deep consequences of witchcraft accusations, and the "official" practices of professional (male) "witch doctors."

6. Robert Rapley. *Witch Hunts: From Salem to Guantanamo Bay.* Montreal: McGill-Queen's University Press annotated edition, 2007. Rapley provides a comparative historical analysis of witch hunting as a social practice, distinct from witches and witchcraft as real people and institutions. His study identifies patterns in social and cultural context across current and historical societies (ranging from the sixteenth through the twenty-first centuries) in which fear of witches emerges as a crucial social dynamic.

7. Jenn Sims, ed. *The Sociology of Harry Potter: 22 Enchanting Essays on the Wizarding World.* Allentown, PA: Zossima Press, 2012. A series of academic essays that place themes, events, and characters from J.K. Rowling's novels in the context of current issues and theoretical orientations (such as those concerning identity, technology, and social inequality) in the field of sociology.

THE REAL WITCHES OF TODAY

A s we saw in the previous section, the lion's share of witchcraft beliefs around the world remain squarely in the domain of accusations and ideology. Witches, in this respect, may be explained as one effect of collective fear and a drive to explain misfortune and suffering. Because these issues are universal, we might well expect witchcraft, too, to exist everywhere as a traditional form of explanation. In some ways, it does indeed exist on a global level—at least insofar as all people everywhere need to make sense of the senseless, and often do so by appealing to transcendent systems of knowledge and causation, and the religious institutions that channel them.

Still, if we ask "average" Americans what they imagine is meant by the terms witches and witchcraft, most people are unlikely to respond in terms of such abstractions. Rather, Americans raised from the post–World War II baby boomer culture and beyond draw on images of the witch coming in equal measures from biblical exposition, classic literature, historical stereotypes, and more recent strains of popular culture (especially in cinema and television). In the bible, the notorious Witch of Endor (First Book of Samuel, chapter 28:3-25) provides a fitting nemesis for contemporary "Bible-believing" Christians (at least twenty-eight percent of U.S. adults, according to the 2014 Gallup Values and Beliefs poll). But even if one isn't exposed from the pulpit to a naturalized vision of the evil-doing hag, the canon of English literature features a triad of similar creatures immortalized by William Shakespeare in his play, *Macbeth*. The "weird sisters" of Shakespeare's imagination were most immediately inspired by the contemporary work of historian Raphael Holinshed on Great Britain and Ireland in the late sixteenth century. They were doubtless also grounded in widespread medieval and early modern fears of Christian society under attack—from raging epidemics and undiagnosed disease, the distant yet terrifying specter of Islam, the unpredictable ebb and flow of natural disasters (for instance, earthquakes, floods, crop blights, sudden deep freezes), and—from the late fifteenth century if not before—the mutual demonization of Christian sects within Europe itself and the devastating wars this internal conflict spurred. The legacy of the 1692 Salem persecutions and images of the witch drawn from these sources have been supplemented by popular culture that seems endlessly obsessed with witchcraft as entertainment—from the popular television series *Bewitched* and *Charmed* to *The Wizard of Oz, The Blair Witch Project,* and the *Harry Potter* series of books and films. These strands of culture have at least two things in common: 1) that the line between how Americans define magic as opposed to witchcraft is easily blurred; and 2) that witches are flesh-and-blood people who are up to no good. This second is a long way from the anthropological notion that witches and witchcraft are in reality a form of logic that explains misfortune, and we would be missing something in this volume if I did not attempt to treat the phenomenon of the witch as "real" in the everyday sense of this word.

As it happens, there is a solid basis for this discussion, although the particulars are probably not what most Americans imagine. In fact, many scholars of "new religious movements" (a.k.a. NRMs or alternative religions) devote much of their careers to the study of various strains of contemporary witchcraft. At the risk of overgeneralization, NRMs are religions that have come into existence in the context of (and often in response to) various problems associated with what historians call "late modernity"—an epoch that is a complex outcome of, among others, new forms of industry and flows of goods, services, and personnel; complex forms of social stratification; deepening and expansive urbanization; and the fragmentation of identities through digital and modern communication and entertainment. These problems may generally be glossed by the term "social anomie"—that is, a widespread rupture between the world as it is promised and expected, and the real world as it confronts people in the experience of life. Although the term new religious movement implies a clean break with some past religious form, this is seldom the case. Most American NRMs build on either conventional world religions such as Christianity (taking the form of new denominations and sects) or on the traditional religions of immigrant communities (for instance, branches of Buddhism and Hinduism brought by immigrants from the mid-twentieth century). Other NRMs (for instance the Raëlians, Heaven's Gate, and—especially—the Church of Scientology) find new meaning in hybrids of science and science fiction, often imbued with innovations proclaimed by a charismatic founder-leader. Still others, such as those discussed in articles in this section (Wicca and Satanism), derive ideas from global mythology and the occult to provide a basis for religious commitment and ritual; they also provide a model and justification for the practice of witchcraft. So, exactly who are these flesh-and-blood witches that dwell among us?

Although space precludes lengthy discussion of these groups, it's useful to point out a few general features. The terms Wicca and Neopagan may be used to gloss an eclectic range of groups whose members share some (but not all) transcendent beliefs, activities, and values. The word Wiccan itself is derived from an Old English word related to the verb "bend" and associated with objects that bed and twist, such as tree branches. Diverse Neopagan cultures venerate a great variety of transcendent beings, many of which are drawn from Celtic, Scandinavian, Near Eastern, Hindu, and Native American mythology. Practitioners assume a ubiquitous power at work in the natural universe that can be manipulated by all people to achieve real-world objectives (note that this is the traditional definition of magic discussed above). As Brennan discusses in relation to English Wiccans, such objectives are typically of a personal nature and patently benign: Wiccans and other Neopagans seek things like health, prosperity in jobs and romance, and protection for their children. Individuals who do so must be of a harmonious mindset and disposition, however, in relation both to the natural world around them and to the universal properties of male and female—symbolic of the powers of procreation and fertility.

Modern witchcraft's generally peaceful objectives and practices do not preclude objections from religious traditionalists, however, who fear "occult" forces and the waning influence of Christian tradition. Critics of Wicca have also been known to espouse a kind of cultural snobbery in which the "strange" ritual activities, unconventional dress, and mystical beliefs are something of an embarrassment. This type of reaction is illustrated in this section by Baker's profile of Christian Day—a Salem "warlock" who has become something of a local business mogul, much to the chagrin of both non-pagans and serious Wiccans alike. The disdain shown by the latter group towards Day reveals something of the complexity of modern witchcraft, in that anyone who seeks to profit from the religion (especially by cashing in on clichés and cartoonish ideas about witches) is deserving of contempt. In sum, these two articles provide a vision of Neopaganism that is both diverse and eclectic.

Much the smaller of the two Neopagan strands discussed in these articles, Satanists, too, claim to have access to the powers inherent in the natural universe. In contrast to Wiccans, for whom an ethic of "do no harm" is central to their creed, Satanists embrace a philosophy of what might be called enlightened selfishness. For the Satanists, the most important feature of the human experience is carnality—the animalistic impulse to indulge all wants and cravings without concern for traditional religious doctrine and moral teaching. These, Satanists believe, are truly immoral institutions that prevent human beings from living out their true potential as earthly creatures. The majority of religious people, so the argument goes, are foolish, delusional, or insufficiently strong to stand up to such powerful institutions. This is why Satanism (which is embedded in a variety of occult traditions) appeals to true individualists; those unafraid to pursue their human vocation. At times, as the article by Stuart makes clear, Satanists are not afraid to be provocative. In enacting their "pink mass" over the grave of a notoriously conservative Christian's mother, members of the New

York–based Satanic Temple managed to both enrage residents of a small Mississippi town and make a nationally felt political statement about the separation of church and state and gay rights. Subsequent assertions that the provocateurs would be arrested rang hollow, and were perhaps designed more for impression management than to describe real law enforcement activity. That the Satanic Temple's witchcraft ritual—apparently designed to magically turn the deceased "gay for all eternity"—was taken seriously by frightened townsfolk speaks volumes about continuing twenty-first-century perceptions that witchcraft is the Devil's work. Similar fears were doubtless stoked (at least for some) by the same institution the following year when Temple members unveiled plans to erect a statue of Baphomet (a horned goat-man symbol embraced by many Satanists) on the grounds of the Oklahoma state legislature—right next to a monument to the Ten Commandments. This unlikely pairing—intended to reinforce a sense that US religion is not "established," and that what was permissible for one should be permissible for all—made the Satanic Temple an unlikely key player in the ongoing debate between partisans of "Christian America," on one hand, and defenders of separation of church and state, on the other. What Temple members had not anticipated was an outpouring of public sympathy for their position—even from Christians concerned with the implications of any single religion's influence on the institutions of state.

As the articles in this section make clear, the witches studied by NRM scholars are hardly the mysterious hags of Shakespearian drama. Rather, they are individuals who create new forms of religious expression modelled on a wide variety of beliefs about the transcendent world. Many seek to revive what they view as "traditional" visions of who witches are and what witchcraft power was all about *before* they were tarnished by Christian moralizing and absolutism. Modern witches, in this regard, exist in the hundreds of thousands and are scattered around the world (although the major groupings thus far studied are linked to European peoples and diasporas). In contrast to the dread nightmares of societies, past and present, for whom witches were an imagined threat to individuals and communities, most members of contemporary witchcraft communities assert their benign status and generally claim a right to practice their faith in the face of much social ostracism and misunderstanding. The articles in section six provide us with a glimpse into a world of unconventional religious practices that, when examined in detail, look fairly familiar in terms of what they offer observers of human spirituality more broadly.

||||||||||||||||||||||||||||||||||||||||||||||||||||||||||||

PAGANS ARE ON THE MARCH

But Are They Harmless Eccentrics or a Dangerous Cult?

ZOE BRENNAN

Dressed in long, hooded cloaks, the women stand in a circle around an iron cauldron.

The chief witch sweeps her broom around the coven, making their circle a sacred space.

A candle is lit, incense is burnt, and spells are mixed in the cauldron.

These are the witches of Weymouth, the latest foot soldiers in the march of paganism in Britain. And this ceremony marks the festival of Samhain—the turning of the year from light to dark.

The Dorset women were last week hailed by the BBC as figureheads of "a reinvented religion," as the corporation's news channel devoted considerable airtime to the festival.

At the same time, it emerged that the Metropolitan Police has produced a diversity handbook offering advice on handling witches and pagans.

Officers are advised not to panic if they encounter a blindfolded person in the nude with their hands tied together. The book reassures them, "This is in accordance with ritual and has the full consent of the participant."

The police are also told to avoid touching a witch's *Book of Shadows*, or spellbook, and not to handle the ceremonial dagger known as an athame.

But it's not only the BBC and the police getting clued up. Druidism has just been given official recognition as a religion by the Charity Commission—with the tax exemptions and other "rights" that follow.

Jailed druids are now allowed to take twigs, or "magic wands," into their prison cells, and are being given official days off prison work to worship the sun.

Critics say that this growing acceptance of primitive beliefs as a new faith undermines our social values.

Mike Judge, spokesman for the Christian Institute, says, "The BBC down-plays Christianity and up-plays paganism which is unreflective of British society. It creates an atmosphere where it's OK to marginalise Christians."

He adds, "When it comes to granting pagans rights, this is surely a case of political correctness gone mad.

"Some people are more equal than others when it comes to the equality agenda, and it seems Christians are always at the back of the queue.

"We are abandoning the values that make us who we are. You can't chip away at the foundations without the whole structure coming down.

"What have pagans ever done? Historically, they produce unstable, violent societies—is that what we want?"

So is paganism really on the march in Britain? And even if it is, why are the BBC and the liberal Left establishment suddenly suggesting that it should be taken seriously—even to the extent of putting it on an equal footing with Christianity and other religions?

For an answer I turned initially to those women in the Dorset field. The leader of the coven is Diane Narraway, who teaches courses in tarot and witchcraft.

One of her congregation, 35-year-old teaching assistant Anouska Ireland, explained what they do. "We sometimes use the cauldron to mix spells, perhaps for the purpose of healing."

Meanwhile, Sarah Sanford, a mother of three, uses witchcraft to protect her children.

She says, "When they are going to school I'll do a protection spell for them, so they get through the day all right."

Another Weymouth witch is Holly Syme, who says her incantations serve very practical purposes.

"You do a money spell, or you do a happiness spell, and it's giving you the motivation to go out there and do what you want," she says. "And it makes you feel better."

Some might be concerned that small children were in attendance at the Samhain ceremony—the footage showed a young girl clutching a teddy—but Ronald Hutton, professor of history at the University of Bristol and the acknowledged U.K. expert on paganism, witchery, and druids, says that witchcraft is benign, adding, "Unless you believe in evil spirits, which I don't."

Paganism is a blanket term for the worship of multiple deities, along with their own mythologies and rituals.

Modern-day pagans draw on Celtic imagery, and often worship the occult.

There are a bewildering number of pagan strands, from druids—who believe themselves to be proponents of the ancient faith of pre-Christian Britain—to wiccans, modern witches who wear a five-pointed star, and shamans who engage with the spirits of the land.

Then there are heathens, worshipping the gods of the north European tribes, including Thor, and the neo-pagans—essentially new-age eco-warrior types.

Central to them all is the idea of a divine force inherent in nature. Prof Hutton says there are up to quarter of a million practising pagans in Britain.

Only 40,000 are registered on the official census, but in the mid-Nineties, he estimated that there were around 120,000 "active engagers" in paganism, a number he believes could have doubled since.

To put that figure in perspective, there are 144,500 Buddhists, according to 2001 figures, and the registered Jewish population numbers 259,000.

The Pagan Federation, which aims to represent all "followers of a polytheistic or pantheistic nature-worshipping religion," claims the number of adherents has reached the 300,000 mark—putting them on a par with the Sikhs.

Indeed, an increasing number of pagans are turning to Stonehenge as their spiritual home, with at least 30,000 celebrating the summer solstice there.

Astonishingly, around 100 members of the Armed Forces now classify themselves as pagans, and a further 30 as witches.

There are thought to be about 500 pagan police officers. A Pagan Police Association has even been set up to represent those who 'worship nature and believe in many gods'.

To the consternation of many, they have been given the right to take days off to perform rituals, such as leaving food out for the dead, dressing up as ghosts and casting spells, or celebrating the sun god with what news reports have described as "unabashed sexuality and promiscuity.'"

So why are Britons reaching out to ancient divinities? Is paganism filling a spiritual void left by the marginalisation of Christianity?

Certainly it seems so. There is even a new Pagan message community on the most middle-class of websites, Mumsnet.

One mother writes, "For the equinox I think I will do something in relation to having a white candle and a black candle. I'd also like to bid farewell to the light out of doors but I'm not sure if those lantern things that float up to the sky are eco or not."

Each spring, more people join the Pagan Pride Parade in London, dressed in velvet robes and carrying broadswords and shields, their heads garlanded in wild flowers.

Prof. Hutton says that paganism is growing in popularity because it addresses modern ills.

"It is gives a sense of connectiveness to the land and to our remote ancestors, both of which we lack in modern life," he says.

"It is also feminist, in that it gives women at least an equal role, unlike most other religions.

"It is environmentally friendly, and regards the natural environment as sacred. It has a powerful personal ethic, which could be described as individualism. It suits the free spirited in that you don't have to do much. It is a back-garden religion."

Undemanding in a moral sense, and with no rigid sense of responsibility, values or right and wrong, it seems to be a perfect religious mish-mash for our times.

And what is the Church of England's view? Asked whether the Church sees the rise of paganism as a good or bad thing, a spokesman says rather feebly, "We wouldn't comment on that."

Ian Haworth from the Cult Information Centre is more outspoken, however. He says, "Paganism does fit under the umbrella of the occult, and that brings concerns.

"Many cults use the occult to brainwash people.

"There are several pagan groups we are concerned by in Britain, they are operating as cults. Paganism is not necessarily harmless."

Keen to find out more about the pagans in our midst, I post messages on several pagan social networking sites on the internet.

Several responses are defensive. Nicola Kerr, from Falkirk, Scotland says, "I will just say this. 'Normal' pagans are everywhere. Living quiet and industrious lives well under the radar of the media.

"We are soldiers, civil servants, teachers, housewives, accountants, university lecturers, farmers, bakers, child-minders, historians, policemen and women, forestry workers, sailors, gardeners, call centre workers, office clerks, dancers and shop workers.

"We live our lives quietly, paying taxes, working hard, loving our families, donating to charities, being part of the fabric of society.

"Next time you are in a public place, consider that some of the people around you may well be Pagan.

"In 99.9 percent of cases you'll never know that they are because they look, and are, normal."

Those living near ancient sites no longer believe paganism is harmless, however.

They complain of pagans ransacking sites for souvenirs, scrawling graffiti on ancient stones, and leaving clothing, beer cans and wiccan effigies littered behind them.

One critic, from Wiltshire, says of pagan activity at nearby Avebury, Silbury Hill and Stonehenge, "These people are entitled to their beliefs and pursuits, they are entitled to dress like '60s hippy throwbacks, and make a lot of noise with drums.

"All I ask is that when they go they take with them their rubbish, tat, paraphernalia, and imposed beliefs and leave our ancient sites tidy and tranquil once more.

"Druids and pagans have no claim on these sites. Britain's historic ancient monuments are for all.

"I for one do not appreciate the arrogant minority shoving their beliefs in my face."

For her part, Diane Narraway of the Weymouth coven will not be drawn into any discussion on the rise of paganism in Britain.

She explains that she is fed up with the attention given to her rituals as a witch.

Lea Jackopson, a pagan from Portland, Dorset, explains that most devotees practise their "faith" without show and are keen not to attract undue attention.

She says, "Paganism is very fragmented in Britain. There are lots of different groves, which are pagan groups or covens. They meet for a 'moot' in a sacred place, in a field, or in someone's living room.

"You go to one about once a month, and share poems and call on the spirits."

She adds, "I don't cast spells or wear robes. I want to live in unity with nature.

"It is a harmless religion with no secrets. The pagans who creep about in disused churches and woodland glades are giving paganism a bad name. The hat-wearing cauldron-stirrers are putting people off."

Nevertheless, they exist. I spoke to one, who would not be named.

She says, "I belong to a coven in Cornwall. We do hold moots in graveyards. Paganism demands that we find the bones of our ancestors in order to commune with their spirits.

"We drink the ancient honey beer mead, and carry out midnight vigils, dancing round the graves.

"Sometimes we'll have the Stag Lord there, with his antlers, representing the Celtic divinity.

"Believe me, paganism is going from strength to strength in Britain. It will take over as newer religions like Christianity die out."

III

SALEM WARLOCK BLENDS BUSINESS WITH SORCERY

BILLY BAKER

C hristian Day used to have a reliable wand guy.

Day is a practicing witch—he prefers the term warlock—but the magic wands were not for personal use.

Instead, he sold the wands in his witch shops in Salem.

One day, he happened to mention to the witch who made the wands for him that his best wand customers were not actual witches, but the parents of children who were into *Harry Potter*.

That's when the wand-maker cut him off, appalled that his fine magical instruments were being used as toys by children.

For Day, such clashes come with the territory when you're trying to become Salem's mogul of the occult.

In the "Witch City," there has long been a tension between the practicing witches who flock to the city and their religion's Halloween-friendly version that is for sale along tourist-heavy Essex Street. Between those two worlds sits Christian Day, the most polarizing figure in the "magical community."

Day has established himself as the high priest of commercial witchery in Salem, the builder of a business empire that includes two witch shops, Hex and Omen; a tour company; a popular book; an elaborate Witches Ball; and The Festival of the Dead, an October-long event that includes speakers and séances and a pop-up psychic parlor set up inside the mall.

The point of all this, Day insists, is not simply to make money, as his critics argue. It's about putting witches to work; he has 20 year-round employees and as many as 50 during the Halloween season, and he says that income helps sustain the witch economy and keep the doors open for the serious practitioners. He could not survive, he said, selling potions alone.

His detractors, a whole coven of them, resent his melding of the occult with the "oh, cute" and his ever-growing commercial reach.

"Some people criticize me for being too commercial to the non-magical community," Day said, "but the mystic and the shaman have always been the beacon of magic for those who didn't understand magic."

Mixed into this brew is Day's grandiose persona. He is known for riding around Salem, in his full witch regalia, on a Segway. He promotes himself as "the World's Best-Known Warlock" on his website. And he is known for dishing out cutting cruelty when he feels attacked by a critic.

"His wands were the basic whittle jobs," he said of the wand-maker who cut him off. "I don't think he would have the talent to make brooms."

For years, Lorelei Stathopoulos was one of Day's biggest critics. "He can be so snippy, snarky, and disrespectful," she said of their clashes. But Stathopoulos, the owner of Salem's oldest witch shop, Crow Haven Corner, found herself siding with Day a few years ago in a fight with the city for more licenses for psychic readers. It was then, she said, that she realized they were on the same team, battling a not-so-hidden faction in Salem that would simply like the whole witch thing to go away.

Now Stathopoulos considers Day one of her closest friends, and sees in him a person who is working incredibly hard, under incredible criticism, to nudge the witch community into something approaching public acceptance.

"One of the biggest things I've done is prove to the rest of the Salem business community that I wasn't just another crazy in black clothes," Day likes to say.

Day, who is 44, came to the business of witchcraft somewhat late in life. He was born in neighboring Beverly "on Christmas Day to a mother named Mary." He moved to Salem when he was 4, and said he grew up as "the weird, terribly shy kid that got picked on." At age 17, he bought his first deck of tarot cards. The following year, he became a practicing witch.

But when it came time to choose a career, Day initially went the traditional route, working in marketing and advertising in Boston until his early 30s, when he came to realize he wanted to live "a magical life full time." He and his best friend, a fellow witch named Shawn Poirier, revived the Witches Ball, then started Festival of the Dead in 2003.

Poirier was the face of the brand, Day said, while he was the business brains, and said their goal was "to create the kind of events we would want to go to." But in 2007, Poirier died, and Day said he was forced to assume both roles, publicly, to a chorus of critics.

"There's not a crime I haven't been accused of on social media," Day said.

And while he argues much of it is born of petty jealousy, there is no doubt that the constant criticism stings him, the endless parade of witches who wish failure on him ... and may even go further.

Last October, he had a spectacular crash on his Segway when one of the wheels magically flew off, as if an occult hand had reached down from above and removed it. Or he hit a curb too fast.

But Day has not backed off on his ambition—he and his Segway have become familiar sights in New Orleans, where he recently opened a witch shop and is planning a festival. And he has not shied away from attention. As he walked down Essex Street recently in a flowing black cloak, black eye makeup, black everything, he basked in the double-takes.

By his side was his fiancé, Brian Cain, a fellow male witch who was similarly dressed. The two will be married next month in a "Warlock Wedding" at Hammond Castle in Gloucester.

They were on their way to the home of Laurie Cabot, the woman who trained Day in witchcraft. Technically, they were going to pick up some "magic spell cords" that Cabot was making for one of Day's shops. But Day always hopes to pick up something else from Cabot: approval.

As they entered her home, Cabot, who is in her 80s, was sitting behind a desk in a black cloak, the hood pulled back to reveal a white mane of hair and the now-iconic swirl tattoo on her left cheek.

The desk was covered in jars of potions, and Day went silent as Cabot dipped a paintbrush into one of the jars and ran it across a leather strap to "charge the spells" she had written on it.

"There's a lot of people who will say he's too commercial, but they said the same thing about me," said Cabot, who began, to much public criticism, the modern era of witchcraft in Salem in the 1970s, hundreds of years after the infamous Salem witch trials of the 1690s.

"But to teach the public, you have to be visible," she said as she dipped the brush again. "Being the most visible witch is the major role."

Day looked on silently, the directive clear, his eyes in a faraway place as if he was lost in a spell.

||||||||||||||||||||||||||||||||||||||||||||||||||||||||||||||||

POLICE SAY THEY PLAN TO ARREST SATANIC TEMPLE MEMBERS WHO PROTESTED WESTBORO BAPTIST CHURCH

HUNTER STUART

Police are preparing to arrest members of a Satanic organization who held a protest ritual earlier this month at a Meridian, Miss., graveyard.

The controversial ritual, called a "pink mass," was carried out by New York-based organization The Satanic Temple and involved gay couples kissing over the grave of Catherine Johnston, the mother of Westboro Baptist Church founder Fred Phelps. The ritual, held at Magnolia Cemetery in Meridian, Miss., was intended to "turn" Johnston gay for all eternity.

But now cemetery owner Bill Arlinghaus is looking to press charges, and Meridian police say they are currently putting together affidavits and warrants in preparation for an imminent arrest of those who performed the ritual, local ABC affiliate WTOK-TV reports.

Meridian Police Department Capt. Dean Harper told the station that the charges being considered are trespassing, indecent exposure and malicious mischief. The indecent exposure charge is likely related to a Satanic Temple spokesman, who goes by the name Lucien Greaves, laying of his penis on Johnston's grave.

Neither Arlinghaus nor the Meridian Police Department immediately responded to requests for comment from The Huffington Post.

However, since the targets of the arrest warrants live in New York City, Harper's talk of apprehending them may just be symbolic. On the phone Monday morning, Greaves did not seem worried about being arrested.

"I think the police captain is trying to allay the fears of the local people," he told HuffPost, adding his group has "no ill will at all" toward the people of Meridian and "regret[s] if they caused them any consternation."

Greaves also questioned the charge of trespassing, saying the cemetery was ungated and the group had visited in the afternoon, during a time when other people could be seen walking about the gravestones.

On its website, the Satanic Temple says the ritual, which was held July 14, was held as a show of support for legal equality for same-sex couples. The group says the idea for the ritual protest came after the Westboro Baptist Church threatened to protest the funerals of victims of the Boston Marathon bombing.

‖‖

SATANIC TEMPLE LEADER "VERY HAPPILY SURPRISED" BY SUPPORT FOR OKLAHOMA MONUMENT

CARLA HINTON

The emails and letters that have poured in to a New York satanic organization in the last few weeks are not exactly what the group expected, a spokesman said.

Spokesman Lucien Greaves said the Satanic Temple of New York has received much correspondence from people who say they are not Satanists but they still support his group's proposal to install a goat demon monument at the Oklahoma Capitol.

In fact, Greaves said, some of them are Christians.

"It's really the best I could hope for. The response has been remarkable, amazing," Greaves said during a recent telephone interview.

"I couldn't have hoped for this magnitude of positive response, but I'm really moved by it. I'm happy and encouraged by people. We're getting emails from people who are Christians who feel comfortable reaching out to us and supporting it."

The New York-based Satanic Temple caused a stir earlier this month when it unveiled designs for a 7-foot-tall statue of Satan that it is proposing to be placed alongside a Ten Commandments monument on the grounds of Oklahoma's Capitol.

The artist's rendering of the statue that was provided by the temple features Satan as Baphomet, a goat-headed demon with horns, wings and a long beard.

The proposal has yet to be considered because the Oklahoma Capitol Preservation Commission has placed a moratorium on considering any such requests while a lawsuit in opposition of the Ten Commandments monument is making its way through the courts. The Oklahoma chapter of the American Civil Liberties Union has sued to have that monument removed on the basis that it violates the separation of church and state.

In the meantime, Greaves said he feels his organization is presenting itself well, judging from the non-Satanists who have felt comfortable enough to approach the group through correspondence.

He said it could mean that many of them are not buying into the myths about Satanism, such as that all Satanists are "homicidal maniacs" or sacrificing animals.

"They are starting to look past the labels to see what we're actually doing and what we actually stand for. I am surprised, but I'm very happily surprised," Greaves said.

"We've gotten a flood of emails from more Oklahomans who stand behind this project and are willing to support it—sign a petition, sign a waiver, you know, help establish our standing or help in any way they can," he said.

"We've heard some criticism that we don't serve Oklahoma values, and I think there is no monolithic voice of Oklahoma values. There is a diverse population in Oklahoma like there is anywhere else, and it's simply ignorant to claim that there is one uniform voice of Oklahoma that can be spoken through any particular politician's narrow view."

'Plurality of voices'

Greaves said the Satanic Temple was contacted by its members in Oklahoma to spearhead the monument project.

Greaves said they believe that if the Ten Commandments monument is allowed to stay, other monuments such as the satanic statue also should be allowed. Other requests for monuments at the Capitol have been made by an animal rights group, the satirical Church of the Flying Spaghetti Monster and a Hindu leader in Nevada.

The satanic monument's supporters, including those who are not Satanists, also believe in this principle, Greaves said.

"This has definitely captured the imagination of a lot of people," Greaves said.

"There's no small number of individuals. Granted, a lot of those individuals who reached out, with emails prefaced by 'I don't consider myself a Satanist but …' or even 'I'm a Christian, however…', but they understand the value in upholding this constitutional freedom of religion and freedom of speech—the principle that we don't discriminate based on race, religion or creed, and that if you open up the public domain to one voice, you have to allow a plurality of voices and that's really what we're founded upon."

Discussion Questions

1. Why is modern paganism problematic for some non-pagans in U.S. and European society?
2. What kinds of magical power are manipulated by modern witches, and for what purposes?
3. According to the article, how do modern pagans blend their beliefs and economic activities?
4. How do non-Satanic varieties of paganism compare with Satanism and Satanic activities?
5. What has the public and law enforcement response been to the recently raised profile of Satanism? Is this a positive development, or not, for U.S. society?

Further Readings

1. Helen A. Berger, ed. *Witchcraft and Magic: Contemporary North America*. Philadelphia: University of Pennsylvania Press, 2011.
   This textbook introduces students to current forms of witchcraft activity in North America. Most especially, contributors offer analyses of such Neopagan religions as Wicca, Satanism, African Caribbean traditions, Neo-Nazi religion, and a variety of occult groups. Berger's volume is very useful for any student desiring a wide-ranging and jargon-free primer on the anthropology and social history of modern witchcraft religions.
2. Brian P. Levack, ed. *The Witchcraft Sourcebook*, Second Edition. New York: Routledge, 2015.
   This volume features a wide range of historically significant essays and documents (many of which are original sources) concerning mainly European and Euro-American varieties of belief in witches and witchcraft activities. These include trial records, theological

and demonological sermons, and accounts of medieval and early modern witch hunts.

3. James R. Lewis, ed. *Magical Religion and Modern Witchcraft*. Albany, NY: SUNY Press, 1996.

Lewis's now-classic ethnological and historical portrait of contemporary witchcraft beliefs and practices covers a wide swath of the Neopagan world, from goddess and nature-focused spiritualities to Odinism and fascination with the occult. In contrast to similar scholarly volumes, he devotes extensive discussion to the connections and divergences between Christian and Neopagan ethics and worldview.

4. Per Faxneld and Jesper Aa. Petersen, eds. *The Devil's Party: Satanism in Modernity*. Oxford University Press, 2012.

A comprehensive and challenging collection of historical and sociological essays that delve in to the murky, diverse, and often misunderstood world of Satanism and Satanists. Essays focus on such topics as the emergence of Satanic practice in the 1960s U.S. counterculture, the progressive development of Satanic activities in the emerging world of online cultures, and the fringe connections between esoteric Satanism and extreme right-wing political groups.

5. David Waldron. *The Sign of the Witch: Modernity and the Pagan Revival*. Durham, NC: Carolina Academic Press, 2008.

This study investigates the origins of contemporary ideas about the Western witch, illuminating the changing character of this symbol from early modern centuries through the contemporary era. Waldron's analysis culminates in exploration of the Neopagan and Wiccan religions of recent decades, which he shows to have transformed the earlier sinister symbolism of witchcraft into something more in keeping with postmodern culture.

INDEX

A

abortion 8, 15
Africa 62, 93, 110, 115–116, 134–135
apocalypse/doomsday 47, 53, 56–57
Atheism 29–30, 36–37

B

babies 73–74
Baphomet 142, 157
Bible 15, 56, 110, 138
Big Bang 44
Book of Shadows 145
Britain/England 22, 31, 93, 125, 134, 138, 145–149

C

Caribbean 62, 102–103, 160
children 19, 21–22, 26, 64–65, 67, 74, 77–80, 82, 98, 108, 111, 115–118, 125, 129–131, 133, 140, 146, 151
Christianity xi, xiii, 4, 11, 13, 23, 61, 103, 111, 115–116, 122, 140, 146–147, 149

church x, 1–4, 8–9, 11, 13, 18, 21–22, 25–30, 32, 34–35, 36–38, 46, 67–68, 77–79, 82, 89–90, 111–112, 115–118, 121–123, 125–127, 129, 131, 134, 140, 142, 148–149, 155–156, 158
collective effervescence 64
creationism 28, 40
crucifix(es) 8, 21–23

D

death/the dead 1, 25, 42, 45, 91, 99, 107, 113, 116, 119–120, 122, 133, 147, 151–152
Devil 38, 89, 108, 112, 122–123, 125, 130, 134, 142, 161
Dracula 87, 104
Druidism/Druids 145–146, 149

E

Europe 8, 21–23, 36–37, 71, 83, 87, 111, 122, 139
evangelicalism 15, 38, 56
evolution 27–28, 43–44, 47–48, 57, 79

exorcism/exorcists ix, 89, 112, 115, 117–118, 121–123, 125, 129–130, 134–135

F

France 8, 22–23, 36, 119

G

gender/transgender 33–35
ghosts 2, 41, 50, 56, 88, 90–91, 131, 147
God x, xiii, 3, 9, 15, 17–19, 22, 26–27, 31–35, 37, 41, 43–44, 47, 56, 78–79, 107, 112, 118, 130–131

H

Haiti 62–63, 86, 103, 109–110, 119–120, 134–135
Harry Potter 60, 62–63, 65, 88, 112, 129–131, 134, 136, 139, 151

I

Islam/Muslims xi, 4, 8–9, 21, 23, 36, 138
Italy 21–23, 37, 125, 127–128

L

Latter-Day Saints Church/Mormons 9, 33–35, 36–37

M

magic (definition) 60–65
Marilyn Manson 97
Medjugorje 125
Middle-Earth 62

N

new religious movements 139
Nigeria 115–117

O

Obeah 62

P

Pope John Paul II 22, 25–26, 40, 46, 122, 127
Protestantism 14
Puritans 1

Q

Qur'an 9

R

religion (definition) 2–5
Roman Catholicism xi, 36, 89, 134
Russian Orthodox 32

S

Salem persecutions/trials 42, 107–108, 110, 134, 136, 139, 153
Satanic Temple 142, 155–158
Satan/Satanic/Satanism xi, 107–112, 122, 127–130, 134, 140–142, 155–158, 160–161
schools/education xii, xv, 19, 21–23, 28, 40, 43, 48, 82, 106, 115–117
science xi, xiii, 27–28, 40–41, 43–46, 48, 51, 54, 56–57, 61, 64, 78, 80, 84, 89, 111, 140
Scientology 140
secularism/secularization x, xiii, 22
sexuality/homosexuality/heterosexuality 15, 48, 54, 78, 94, 147
Star Wars 63–65, 83
superstition 110, 121

T

Ten Commandments 23, 142, 157–158

U

United States ix–x, 1, 8, 10, 13, 23, 28–29, 36, 38, 60, 77, 80, 86, 93, 102, 106–107, 123

V

vampires xi, 2, 87–88, 90, 93–95, 97–98, 102, 104, 129

Vatican 22, 25–28, 46, 122–123, 125, 128, 130

Vodou/Voodoo xi, 62–63, 103, 109–110, 120

W

Walt Disney/Disneyland 60, 64–65, 69–71, 82

weeping statues 1, 84

Wicca 140–141, 147–148, 160–161

witchcraft (definition) 106–112

Z

zombies/ghouls 42, 51–54, 56, 86–88, 90–91, 102–103

CPSIA information can be obtained
at www.ICGtesting.com
Printed in the USA
LVHW05s0138300818
588541LV00009B/163/P